LEVERAGE

A KEY TO SUCCESS AND WEALTH

RON D. PATE

VP Publishing, LLC
Rocky Mount, North Carolina

Printed in the United States
11 10 9 8 7 6 5 4 3 2
Cover and icons by Liaison Design Group, LLC
VP Publishing, LLC
P.O. Box 4623
Rocky Mount, NC 27803

LCCN 2003117156
ISBN 0-9705793-0-6

To learn more about Ron D. Pate, please visit www.RonDPate.com. For training programs by Ron and his team please visit Key Business Institute, Inc. at www.KeyBI.com.

This book is dedicated to my dad for believing in me and inspiring me to move beyond my comfort zone and reach for my dreams, and for providing me with a tremendous role model of honesty, love, and hard work.

PRAISE FOR *LEVERAGE: A KEY TO SUCCESS AND WEALTH*

"Ron Pate has created a very concise and highly readable explanation of how and why leverage is such a vital factor in building one's financial future ... but, even more than that, this book is a guide to principles which we all need to adopt to live a fulfilling life. I strongly recommend this book, no matter what you choose as your life's mission."

> \- Jeffrey Rich
> Millionaire real estate investor

"This book is packed with 'wealth truth' ... that, when internalized and applied, has the potential to transform one's future. I highly recommend this book!"

> \- Greg Torrance
> Founder, Future Hope Residential, LLC

"I've read Steven Covey and others like him and learned a lot. Ron's book on Leverage embraces some of the same concepts, but offers readers a different construct to view immediate opportunities to leverage opportunities well within their reach."

> \- Dennis Phillips
> Family therapist and investor

CONTENTS

Introduction   ix

Acknowledgements   xv

Guide to Icons   xvii

Chapter 1: What is Leverage?   1

Chapter 2: Time Leverage   23

Chapter 3: Money Leverage   47

Chapter 4: Knowledge Leverage   67

Chapter 5: Wealth Concepts   83

Chapter 6: Risk   131

Chapter 7: Technology and the Information Age   137

Chapter 8: A Strong Foundation   153

Chapter 9: A Call to Action   163

INTRODUCTION

My personal journey of success began approximately two decades ago in the small town of Tarboro, NC. Since that time, I have sought diligently to understand why some people achieve extraordinary success while others fail to realize anywhere near their full potential. In my search, I have studied well over 500 books, over 100 audio courses, and most importantly have had the opportunity to learn first hand from dozens of highly successful role models.

Although financial accomplishment is not itself an indicator of success, many who have reached a point in life where they can, without restriction, focus full-time on pursuing their life purpose have also reached a level of financial freedom uncommon for the vast majority of people. Indeed, because we live in a money driven society, those with the most performing assets tend to have the greatest options, the greatest opportunity to enjoy all that life has to offer, and to do the most good for others. Those who give back the most to society, often tend to be those who have reached the highest levels of financial achievement.

I especially considered those who achieve very high levels of income, levels which seem impossible to most who realize more average yields on their efforts. I found those who realize very high earnings and who accumulate significant assets in surprisingly short periods of time often have similar levels of talent and desire as many of those who never achieve more than average levels of financial accomplishment. Indeed, with regard to most important success factors, the two groups are often very similar.

It turns out there is a very simple, yet very powerful tool which is employed by the wealthy group which is not employed in any appreciable manner by the less wealthy group, and which accounts for a significant portion of the difference in outcomes realized by the two groups. The tool is LEVERAGE. Indeed, if you look carefully at the vehicles and strategies taught by some of the most popular trainers and authors on financial success, it is leverage which drives these vehicles.

For example, one of the reasons long-term investments in real estate tend to yield the highest percentage returns of almost any investment in history is the use of financial leverage. Many large corporations use time and knowledge leverage to generate massive returns, whereas almost all small proprietorships result in only average returns to the entrepreneur. And many new Internet entrepreneurs realize seemingly unbelievable returns on their efforts in surprisingly short timeframes because of their understanding and use of technology leverage.

Most people have heard the word "leverage" but few understand what it really means. Indeed, many think in terms of financial leverage, and while financial leverage is one of the basic forms of leverage used to develop wealth, it is by no means the only form. Indeed, those who realize the greatest outcomes employ not only financial leverage but other forms of leverage as well. Perhaps one of the reasons leverage is so misunderstood is that little intentional effort has been made to clarify and illuminate this powerful tool as a fundamental success principle.

In this book, I introduce you to this powerful concept and through the use of simple examples, help you internalize and shift your thought patterns such that you will, if you so choose, begin to realize ways in your own life to apply leverage for success.

The understanding of leverage, and its application in your own life, will help you magnify your accomplishments, given the talents and resources you currently possess, in truly exciting ways. If you indeed "get it" and understand the insights spread throughout this book then you will undoubtedly begin to succeed in ways you may never have dreamed possible.

Through the proper application of leverage to your existing talents and financial and non-financial assets, you can realize a remarkable growth in your assets and accomplishments. However, the application of leverage in this manner, especially with regard to the development of financial accomplishment, requires that you have the proper mindset. Therefore, this book also discusses numerous important matters which must be understood, explored, and internalized if you are to achieve the maximum success possible. Many of these are presented in the chapter entitled "Wealth Concepts" although there are numerous others carefully woven throughout the text.

To realize the maximum benefit from any particular strategy, one must thoroughly understand, internalize, and learn to apply the core principles behind the strategy. It is no different when considering the application of leverage for success. This book introduces you to the core principles of leverage.

If you've applied all the principles of success you've so diligently studied and still seem to be spinning your wheels, making little progress toward your dreams, leverage may very well be the missing ingredient that places you firmly on the road to realization of your dreams.

Keep in mind as you read the many examples throughout this book that the same concept often applies regardless of the size of the situation, or the amount of money involved. Think beyond the simple examples you'll discover to all the ways the same idea and strategy can be utilized, often in far greater ways than the example shown.

Although you will finish this book quickly, remember it is through repeated reading, and most importantly, application that you will truly benefit from the power of leverage. As you read, make notes freely as you gain personal insights, or as concepts trigger your own genius to emerge. Seek out more information and find ways to apply leverage as often as possible. In looking for more detailed information on the topics discussed, and by seeking ways to apply that which you're learning, you will internalize the concepts and they will become a part of your personal success system.

Above all, commit to use that which you learn or discover by taking action. Knowledge without application generally does little to further you on your success journey. Diligent application of the success principles you learn through study, and more importantly experience, is the only way you will ever realize your true potential.

I wish you the greatest in success.

— Ron Pate

ACKNOWLEDGEMENTS

Any work such as this book requires a diligent effort on the part of numerous people. Please allow me to express my humble gratitude for the help numerous friends and associates have provided in bringing this work to you.

First, I'd like to thank my dad, J.C. Pate, for his inspiration and guidance these many years. Much of the information you see herein was spawned from the principles and attitudes he instilled in me at a very young age. He has continued to be an extraordinary role model through many difficult times, and you would most certainly not hold this book in your hands were it not for him. Daddy, Thank You!

Next, I'd like to thank my loving wife, Lucy, for her tremendous support night after night when I suddenly disappeared to our office leaving my side of the bed cold and abandoned. Your understanding, patience, belief in my mission, and most importantly your love, is so greatly appreciated that words cannot express the depth thereof. Thank you darling. I love you!

I'd like to also express my continued gratitude to James Vick, Mike Corbin, and

Becky Corbin of VP Publishing, for their patience and guidance as I wrote and rewrote the manuscript. Thank you for your continued support to help make this book a reality!

A very special thank you goes to my editor Colleen Bunting, whose detailed and insightful editing brought this book to life.

Finally, I'd like to thank the following associates who graciously took valuable time out of their schedules to share with me ideas for the book and feedback on the initial manuscript, helping to make it the best that it can be. To Drew Ludlow and Matt Young, I offer my sincere thanks for your valuable contribution and support.

— Ron Pate

GUIDE TO ICONS

Throughout this book you will find the following icons in the margins. These indicate an example is shared in the text and point out the specific type of leverage demonstrated in the example.

 Money Leverage

 Knowledge Leverage

 Time Leverage

 Technology Leverage

Chapter One

What is Leverage?

"Give me a lever

and I can move the world."

— Archimedes

THE MISSING INGREDIENT

The ability to become wealthy and to design a personal life of freedom, flexibility, and accomplishment is within everyone's reach. With the many modern advances available to us today, it is possible, by applying even just a small amount of correct knowledge, to become financially independent, and to do so with life balance, enjoyment, and excitement. Why then is it that after having read numerous financial and self-help books, and after having diligently applied lessons learned from countless seminars, that so many fail to ever achieve any measure of wealth and financial accomplishment? What is the missing ingredient that keeps people who apply all the valuable lessons they've learned from reaching their dreams?

While working to achieve my goal of life and financial freedom, I studied and researched diligently to identify this missing ingredient. It turns out the missing ingredient is well known and highly utilized by all who achieve outstanding success. **The missing ingredient is leverage.**

If you read and study popular books and training programs on wealth development and success you'll seldom see the concept of leverage outlined and explained. Many of the topics discussed have leverage as an inherent ingredient in the overall strategy presented, but fail to explain this fundamental principal. Without understanding the underlying principle which is at the root of success strategies you learn, it is difficult to truly internalize the concepts. More importantly, it is difficult to apply the strategies to all areas of your life and business. Indeed, understanding the fundamentals of any given strategy is essential if you wish to use it effectively for maximum success.

The leverage concept is one that can truly change your life. By understanding and utilizing this powerful concept you will complete the puzzle that keeps so many from financial success and life freedom. It is an incredibly powerful tool and when you begin to apply it in your life and business you will be astounded at how new worlds of opportunity will open up to you.

Excellent training materials are readily available today, materials that provide powerful concepts which can lead you to great accomplishment, particularly in the financial realm. In many financial and business success training materials on the market today, the leverage concept is integrally woven throughout, though many may not realize it. It is the clear understanding of this powerful concept that will help put the strategies in these training materials into perspective.

Just one clarifying moment can change your life. If you realize such a clarifying moment with regard to the leverage concept, many blinders will disappear and you'll see what is missing in your strategies and why you may not be realizing the long-term results you desire.

Many courses briefly allude to the power of leverage, but usually in just an isolated fashion. If you study real estate investing, one of my passions, then you'll likely encounter leverage through the use of borrowed money. However, the application of leverage for true long-term wealth development goes much further than this. For many real estate investors the true power of leverage as a long-term wealth development strategy is overlooked. I am convinced it is because the core concept was never internalized and thus leverage was never integrally woven throughout all of their activities.

LEVERAGE DEFINED

As I wrote this book I searched diligently for a crystal clear definition of the leverage concept as applied to the development of wealth and overall life accomplishment. After hours and hours on the Internet and scanning through books likely to contain its definition, I came up empty handed. For example, the dictionary defines leverage as "The action of a lever; mechanical advantage gained by the lever." This obviously offers very little insight into how leverage is used by those who achieve extraordinary wealth and success.

After careful consideration, I arrived at the following definition:

Leverage is a principle whose application allows magnification, without practical limit, of the output realized from a given amount of input.

Let's carefully consider this representation of the leverage concept as used for wealth development and success.

First, leverage, like all powerful strategies responsible for achievement, must be viewed as a tool. Like any tool, if misused or used irresponsibly, leverage can be dangerous. But if used responsibly it is the principle that will complete the other success strategies you learn, especially with regard to wealth development.

Second, the fact that there is no established limit to the magnification of output that the application of leverage can provide explains why some people achieve such extraordinary results in just a few decades, or lately in just a few years. For example, consider the wealth that Bill Gates has generated not only for himself but the thousands of others who have become multimillionaires through the growth of Microsoft Corporation.

This is why it is critical you understand leverage and its use. Many of the concepts taught in mainstream success and wealth training focus on tactical strategies and methods. Leverage is more of a strategic idea and concept. It underlies many of the most successful strategies taught for wealth development and a clear understanding of this powerful concept will open your eyes in a way that will almost certainly, if properly applied, result in rapid changes in your accomplishment, regardless of your field of endeavor.

For example, many books discuss the power of building your own business system, the power of real estate investing, or the power of the Internet to help you achieve financial independence. Leverage is the common element shared by all of these vehicles. In the popular Rich Dad™ series for example, one of the primary differences between the 'B' business ("big business") and the 'S' business ("small business") is the fact that the 'B' business is designed to employ leverage. The principal reason real estate investing results in so many becoming wealthy is that the lending guidelines in our country, as well as real estate laws, are designed to allow maximum use of financial leverage. Likewise the Internet is such an incredible tool for reaching financial independence because of the ability to leverage its structure to reach many people with very little effort. Every one of these vehicles has this one powerful concept as the driver behind its ability to make you wealthy or to otherwise magnify your accomplishment.

LEVERAGE VERSUS USE OF RESOURCES

When discussing the leverage concept, I am often asked about the difference between usage of a resource and leverage.

When you implement leverage, you increase the amount of effective output you realize with the given resource, with little or no increase in the amount of time required to do so.

To clarify this distinction, let's consider a simple example. Assume you hire a company to cut your grass and maintain your yard instead of doing it yourself. If you perform a task with equivalent output or value as you would have received by maintaining the lawn yourself, or if you produce no output of tangible value with the time saved by employing the third party, then you have used a resource but you have not employed leverage. Let's assume you pay $10/hour for the lawn care services and a service takes 4 hours. Assume you would have also taken four hours to perform the same tasks. If you do something which results in $40 of profit or yield in the four hour time frame, then you have indeed used a resource, but the leverage employed is essentially zero. Consider on the other hand that you perform a task during this four hour time frame which results in a profit of $250, and with equivalent effort on your part. Now, you have not only utilized a resource, but you have also leveraged a resource, as the net yield from your four hours is $210, much greater than you would have realized without the use of the lawn care provider.

Understanding and distinguishing between the simple use of a resource and the implementation of leverage in a given situation is essential if you are to harness the power of this concept. Perhaps one way to keep this principle at the forefront of your mind is to understand a characteristic of leverage which I refer to as **resource amplification**.

RESOURCE AMPLIFICATION

Within the context of leverage, resource amplification refers to the increase of effective value of a given resource through the magnified output resulting from the leveraged use of the resource. For example, if you have at your disposal $5,000 to invest in real estate, you can purchase with little difficulty, provided your financial status is sufficient, a performing asset valued at $100,000. Through the use of leverage, you have effectively amplified the value of your available $5000 resource.

Everyone has certain resources at his or her disposal. In order to achieve the greatest results from the use of leverage to magnify the value of your resources, it is very important to distinguish those resources which most warrant amplification. After careful analysis you will most likely find the application of leverage for wealth development and personal or professional accomplishment is best applied to the resources of time, knowledge, money and in today's modern society, technology.

INTERNALIZATION OF CONCEPTS

If you wish to reach extraordinary goals, you must truly internalize and utilize the most powerful concepts at your disposal for the accomplishment of your goals. Thus, application of the leverage concept, and altering your thought patterns to integrate this into your daily life is essential if you wish to truly benefit from the power this tool provides. You must carefully evaluate your daily actions to see how and where you might best apply the leverage concept to help you accomplish more with the same or less effort.

EFFICIENCY AND EFFECTIVENESS

Efficiency, which is based on eliminating waste, is often considered with regard to accomplishing more with less. And while efficiency is a very powerful and useful idea, the amount of gain you can realize from its application is limited. Leverage on the other hand offers the potential for unlimited gain. For example, you can purchase a parcel of real estate with none of your own money and have that real estate provide to you income, effectively resulting in an infinite yield from your financial investment. Understand that leverage can never provide infinite yield on your total input, for in the example cited above you did have to provide some minimal input of time and talent. Because applying leverage can offer yields approaching infinity, leverage application is in a category well beyond simple efficiency. Combine the power of leverage with the power of efficiency (doing things the right way) and with the power of effectiveness (doing the right things) and you truly can realize amazing gains.

APPLICATION REQUIRED

As with any new knowledge obtained, without application, understanding the leverage concept will do you little good.

I remember when I was having dinner at a restaurant in Bradenton, FL with a business associate. When the waitress delivered our meal, Dave and I were discussing how some people achieve high levels of success, while others simply go through life, never making progress toward their dreams. I asked the waitress, a young lady of maybe 18 years of age, if she'd like a suggestion, which if she followed, could change her life forever. She of course said, "Yes!" At that, I briefly explained the leverage concept and suggested she research how to apply it for greater success. I shared with her a quick example, and then she was off to serve the next table. In leaving, she thanked me, and said she'd give it a try. During a subsequent visit to the restaurant I encountered this same individual and asked if she remembered me. After a brief reminder of our conversation she said she did, but admitted she never really looked into what I had advised any further. Don't be like this person who, for whatever reason, avoided one of the very principles which could revolutionize her life and the life of those around her. Instead, take this principle and find ways to apply it in your life.

Let's briefly look at a few examples of leverage in action. Well before the invention of modern hydraulic equipment, the ancient

Egyptians raised stones weighing hundreds of tons with the simple, rudimentary tools available at the time. They used ropes, pulleys, and levers, in a carefully designed arrangement or system, to move tremendous weights with mere human physical power. They used physical leverage.

There are many entrepreneurs who run multiple companies, earning millions of dollars per year, while working no more than 40 hours per week. These individuals leverage the time and knowledge of others, along with various systems that have been designed to allow far greater output and yield from their efforts than they could have achieved on their own. They don't simply use the time and knowledge of others, but rather they do so in a fashion that creates highly leveraged outcomes resulting in their high earnings with only a reasonable input of personal time and effort.

Finally, consider how modern computerized offices can process more information in a day than was processed in the entire world in a full week just a few hundred years ago. Through the power of technology leverage, information processing barriers are constantly being expanded at mind numbing rates.

In fact, there are many examples all around

you every single day. The problem is that most people go through life with mental blinders on, never realizing how so much is accomplished with so little in so many situations, and how it might enable them to achieve extraordinary results in their own lives.

Although physical leverage, with which most people are familiar, is conceptually related to the forms of leverage that can lead you to outstanding success, the ones you need to achieve success and wealth focus on the use of your mind more than physical strength. Indeed, the power of the mind to make you wealthy in today's emerging information age is far greater than you may imagine. If you develop the proper focus, apply the concepts of leverage discussed herein in a win-win fashion that provides value to others, and persist through the initial growth challenges you are likely to encounter, you will realize results in your life that will amaze you.

 Let's look at another example of leverage application. My wife enjoys transcribing medical records on a part-time basis. She is often found at our computer, transcribing doctors' dictated referral letters. Each time a referring doctor's address is to be typed, Lucy just enters a couple of characters, and entire addresses appear instantly. In fact, as she types, whole paragraphs appear with the simple entry of just a few keystrokes. Lucy completes whole pages, as dictated by the doctor, in as little as one minute. This feat is accomplished by understanding the repeated phrases and taking the time once to program them into the computer, so that they can later be inserted with minimal effort. Since Lucy is paid by the number of lines typed, if she has the computer type half the lines with just a few key strokes, she doubles her hourly rate with very little effort. Do you see the leverage here? This activity is still "swapping hours for dollars," but is far better than using no leverage whatsoever.

Many other typists around the country have a similar system, and yet very few realize how this simple concept which they apply daily relates to achieving success and wealth. Leverage is a very simple yet powerful concept and can be applied to any number of situations, ranging from simple examples such as this to those with far greater implications. Indeed, this concept the typists employ, if it served as a seed idea for greater exploration and implementation, and if applied to more significant matters, might lead to remarkable accomplishments in their lives.

Carefully consider your work and home life. Identify at least three activities in which you currently participate where you might be able to apply the leverage concept. Develop strategies for introducing leverage into these activities and TAKE ACTION!

SPOTTING OPPORTUNITIES

Before delving further into this discussion of leverage, let's discuss how you can identify opportunities to employ leverage in your own life.

Contrary to popular misconception, opportunity is everywhere. Most people have the seeds of great success within them, and have for all practical purposes unlimited opportunities to plant those seeds in a way that can result in a rich harvest. They have talents, relationships, and desires which can yield any level of success they might realistically desire. However, most have mental blinders on so they don't recognize, or worse, are never exposed to, this tremendous concept of leverage.

Why do many people go around never realizing the opportunities surrounding them? Believe it or not, just as with habits, it goes back to our mental programming. Allow me to share another real life experience to help you understand how the mind works when it comes to spotting opportunities.

When I graduated from college, I purchased a new Ford Thunderbird, complete with a moon roof, custom wheels, and a premium stereo. I did not decide on the car to buy prior to visiting the dealership, instead allowing my emotions and the helpful salesperson to influence my decision.

Once I found just the right car for me, I considered that I hadn't seen many of this body style on the road. Therefore, I would be unique as well as sporty. After purchasing the car, I left the showroom and immediately headed to the beach, about three hours away, for a celebration weekend. As I drove, I must have seen hundreds of the same model car as my new gem. But where did THEY come from? They hadn't been there before, had they? I was shocked and dismayed that so many other people were driving the same car as I. But why hadn't I noticed all those Thunderbirds on the road before I bought my little beauty?

You see, before I purchased this car, I had no emotional connection to the Thunderbird design. Now that I had an emotional connection with this particular car, my brain began filtering the input I was taking in differently. Suddenly I began to notice the very same cars that I had never noticed before.

Indeed, have you ever noticed how certain things just happen around you without your ever being truly aware of them? That is, you "tune" them out.

Let's suppose you're at home listening to the television. There are noises all around you that you simply tune out. Perhaps you hear but fail to notice the air conditioner compressor kicking in, the squeaking of your rocking chair, or the whirring of your computer fan. But then, when you hear a troubling noise from your little girl in the other room, faint as it may be, you're suddenly on the run.

You see, your brain takes in the vast array of input signals arriving through your senses every moment, and filters them against the things that you consider most important and to which you have the strongest emotional connection. This is a miraculous part of your brain's natural programming contained in a small section of your brain known as the Reticular Activating System.

So, how can you tap into this miraculous feature of your mental programming, coupled with the leverage concept, to move you toward greater success? First and foremost, it is critically important that you really internalize the importance of leverage in helping you achieve your dreams. Study this book, research the concept of leverage on your own, and begin focusing on identifying specific opportunities to take advantage of leverage in your own personal situation. Practice finding and employing leverage first in simple ways, then in more important or complex ways. As you begin seeking leverage opportunities at work, at home, and in every facet of your life, you'll be amazed at how many opportunities exist that you never noticed before! The more you seek and practice leverage, the more it will be internalized and the more your Reticular Activating System will help you find new, powerful, and profitable ways to employ it. Consider for example what truly necessary activities you are doing that could be simplified or automated, or better yet combined with other activities. Perhaps you are currently engaged in activities that could be turned into a system where others are hired to do the work for you. As you read this book, you will have many ideas. Stop and record them.

Think of at least one task you do frequently which does not make maximum use of your skills, and for which you could leverage someone else's time. Develop a strategy for delegating this task to the other person, while employing the same time you would have spent on this task doing something which is more in line with your core skills and which will result, over time, in far greater income than the amount you pay to this person for the performance of this task.

Remember, you must become diligent in looking for leverage opportunities every day, and you must constantly be thinking of how you can use those opportunities for greater personal success.

FORMS OF LEVERAGE

The basic time proven forms of leverage which you can use to achieve outstanding levels of success are time leverage, money leverage, and knowledge leverage. A relatively new and unique player on the scene is technology leverage. You'll see many variations of these in different reference materials, and when you talk with highly successful people. Regardless of what they're called, these concepts form the foundation on which many successful leverage vehicles are built.

Consider celebrities who realize tremendous financial incomes in just a few years. Consider which forms of leverage drive the vehicles responsible for the rapid growth of their income streams. How might you apply one or more of these forms of leverage driven vehicles in your own life?

Let's review these forms of leverage one at a time and see how they can be used to accelerate your progress on your journey of success.

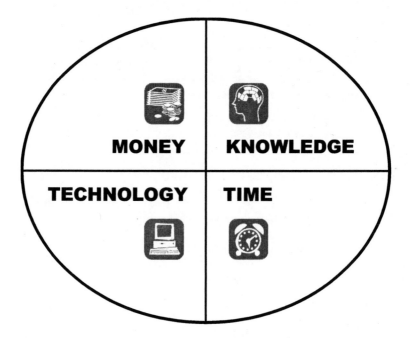

THE LEVERAGE FAMILY

This image represents the four most useful forms of
leverage for the attainment of extraordinary
outcomes, especially financial achievement.
Whenever possible, employ multiple forms of
leverage in combination with one another to
maximize the yield from your efforts.

Chapter Two

Time Leverage

"Time is one of the most precious resources available to us, and yet we continue to treat it as if there were an unlimited supply. To achieve our maximum potential, we must develop a relentless focus on spending our dwindling supply of time in the best way possible, each moment of every day."

— Ron D. Pate

TIME LEVERAGE

Time is limited. You cannot create more of it, you cannot store it, and interestingly enough, you don't even know how much of it you truly have left. You have exactly the same amount of time available to you in a given day as President George Bush or multibillionaire Bill Gates. You in fact have all the time there is. If you are not investing your time effectively and employing time leverage, then you will fail to realize your true potential in life.

To increase the effective amount of time you have with which you can accomplish your dreams, you must utilize the time of other people. Contrary to popular misconception, leveraging the time of others for your own accomplishment is not wrong provided you leverage their time in the right way. As you work with others, always seek to share the knowledge you've gained with them, and always look for win-win opportunities to inspire and move them along on their own journey of success. Never take advantage of others for personal gain. There is sufficient opportunity to go around, and as long as you don't take advantage of people, you will help people in more ways than you can imagine by accomplishing more yourself.

It amazes me how many people go through life working very hard, yet working in a totally linear fashion. When the money gets tight, they think of working longer hours. The concept of leverage is never considered. Yet, this is such a simple concept, and there are for all practical purposes an unlimited number of ways to apply it for great benefit. Don't blindly swap your hours for dollars. Employ time leverage.

If you go through life exchanging your time for a fixed amount of dollars in a typical job, you are guaranteed to be limiting the amount of dollars you can earn. You can't make more hours can you? And regardless of what field you are in, there is a limit to how much you can earn with one hour of your own individual effort. If you're an eye surgeon, then you may earn an average of $400 per hour. If you apply leverage, you could possibly earn $4000 per hour or more for your effort. But as long as you work without employing some form of leverage, you will never realize the highest potential possible from every hour of effort.

Total your income and divide it by the number of hours you spend per year actively generating this income. What is your average hourly income? Would you like to increase this amount? By how much? Consider how to employ leverage to effect this change.

Let's look at an example. As a freelance bookkeeper Dana was earning $25 per hour for her services. Through dedication and a strong customer focus, she had developed a loyal client base, and had as much work as she could personally handle. In fact she was turning work away.

Dana consulted with me on her plans for business growth. She indicated she enjoyed her work, but that she really wanted to increase the amount of money she was investing for retirement. Therefore, she needed to increase her earnings. Dana had two choices. She could earn more with her own time, or she could employ leverage to increase her earnings. She chose to find ways to leverage her time rather than trying to cram more working hours into her already packed schedule.

Dana used the relationships she had established previously in her market to seek out other qualified individuals performing similar work. She approached her contacts and explained the positive results they could realize by teaming up with her to deliver services. Soon she found a qualified professional that would work with her for $18 per hour. Interestingly, the other bookkeeper, Dan, was only charging $16 per hour before Dana approached him, so he was excited at the prospect of working with Dana. She brought Dan on board her team as an independent contractor working under her company name, while at the same time merging his client base into her own. Most of Dan's clients didn't mind, because they knew Dan was worth every penny of the new hourly rate of $25 they would be paying, and they respected Dan's decision to team up with Dana. Dana's new associate no longer had to worry about marketing his services. He instantly became part of a larger organization. Together Dan and Dana began sharing ideas for growth, thus leveraging their mutual expertise.

Dana now was earning $25 per hour for her time and $7 per hour on Dan's time. Assuming Dan was working half as many hours as Dana, Dana was effectively earning $3.50 per hour additional, meaning she had increased her earnings by 14%! But even better, Dana found that their collective expertise exceeded that which she previously had individually. Therefore she was able to increase her pricing from $25 per hour to $30 per hour for the higher end clients with more complex bookkeeping needs, and to simultaneously deliver even greater value to her clients. This is due to her leveraging the knowledge of others, a concept we'll review in more detail later. Through maybe twenty hours worth of effort, and very little initial cost, Dana increased her earnings by over 25%, with very little increase in the amount of hours she worked! Once she had successfully employed this strategy, she began to realize the sky is the limit.

Although this example neglects the administrative costs in terms of time and money that Dana likely incurred from adding another team member, the monetary increases and non-monetary rewards she received are far greater than the costs. This is truly a win-win situation. Both benefited from the power of shared knowledge and experience, as well as the many other advantages of having team members to cover emergencies, vacation, etc. Indeed, this is a highly simplified example of how many multi-billion dollar enterprises started, and it is based on the exact same principle that allows the founders of those multi-billion dollar enterprises to realize the tremendous returns they enjoy.

Let's take this one step further, examining another of the practically unlimited uses of time leverage. As you will note in this and the previous example, most forms of leverage are employed in combination with other forms of leverage, rather than all by themselves.

As any truly successful business owner will tell you, one major secret of business success lies in the development of workable systems that leverage available resources for maximum benefit. Benefits come in many forms, not the least of which is profits. Systems in this context are nothing more than frameworks in which forms of time leverage are employed.

Let's consider McDonald's Corporation. What is the secret that Ray Kroc, founder of McDonald's, recognized that allowed this company to become such a successful enterprise? It's not the hamburger, as you might assume. Instead, it's the power of an excellent system. McDonald's™ has an excellent, easily reproducible system for the delivery of fast food. Likewise, every successful franchisee, in following the carefully designed system of operation, increases the profits of the corporation. Highly refined procedures lead to predictable, consistent output, leveraging the time of many workers with little specialized knowledge to produce massive quantities of food and profits. That's leverage in action.

What skills do you have with which you could develop a system employing some form of leverage to provide products or services in greater and greater quantities with little additional investment of your time, once the system is established? Remember, start small and grow from there.

 Let's consider another simple example of time leverage. Suppose you've obtained your real estate broker's license, allowing you to act on behalf of others as a real estate agent. You're working under a reputable organization, and you have the advantage of national advertising, as well as established forms and systems. If you're familiar with typical real estate offices, you'll realize that you're really your own business, and that you're in a sense renting the name and space of a larger organization.

After a year or two, you find that your client base has grown through word of mouth due to your excellent service and client attention. You are working long hours and seem to have reached the maximum income possible, because you're working in purely linear fashion. Life isn't as fun as it used to be, you know that it is impossible to work harder, and since the market sets the commission rates you earn, you've basically topped out on the earnings scale.

So, what do you do? Well, a first step might be to look at the things you do during a typical day. You'll find there are many tasks you're performing that in turn provide little financial return on investment, but that are indeed necessary. There are many tasks that do not take full advantage of your considerable talent. For example, you regularly send mailings out to your client base, and you find yourself late at night at the kitchen table folding and addressing these mailings.

To take advantage of leverage, you find a knowledgeable assistant, one who is highly motivated and who shares your values. You allow this individual to perform all the tasks in which you do not need to be directly involved. This frees your time for activities that generate a greater return on your invested time, and it allows you to significantly increase your output and income.

As a next step, you might consider starting your own brokerage firm, bringing on not only assistants, but other qualified agents as well. By organizing the team, and obtaining a share of the proceeds from the team members' time, you'll even further increase your use of leverage. Develop systems and methods whereby you teach and empower others on your team to do what it is that you do which makes your clients want to do business with you. Find people with similar values and interpersonal skills as those that make you successful. In essence, duplicate yourself through others.

While you're thinking about this example, consider other ways that leverage could be employed by not only building a real estate business system, but also by combining this with the power of Information Age trends for additional leverage.

Of course, there are many factors involved in each of these examples, but as many successful organizations bear witness, it is a great deal more productive than simply swapping your own hours for dollars in purely linear fashion. Think strategically about how you can spend a little of your time now developing ways to use leverage, thus freeing up substantial amounts of your time later.

GREAT PEOPLE ARE THE KEY

While we're on this topic of time leverage, and more specifically leveraging the time of others by building a team, we need to address a matter that is absolutely critical to success.

When it comes to building a team, you must be very careful whom you add to your team. You must be 100% certain that you get the right people on your team initially, and if you happen to bring on someone that is not right for the team, remove him or her from the team as quickly as possible. Having the wrong people on your team can cause you significant headaches, can damage your reputation, and can most certainly set you back in ways you can't imagine if you've never been there. Remember that just because a person has positive values and means well does not mean he or she is right for your team. Not only does having the wrong people on your team hurt the output of the team, it also hurts the individuals themselves. They cannot reach the success they undoubtedly desire, since the team must ultimately succeed if the individual team members are to realize the maximum success of which they're capable. There are numerous resources available to you to help you screen and evaluate potential team members. Don't be penny wise and pound foolish in finding great people for your team. Be patient in your search, and make sure they're right before bringing them onboard.

Suppose you have an attractive opportunity and you are seeking highly qualified team members to assist you in capitalizing thereon. You want to get to know them before bringing them in as part owners or managers of your organization. For example, since I've been able to achieve fairly significant goals in real estate investing and financial accomplishment, people regularly approach me about teaming up with me in one of my organizations. Last year, Matt, a highly qualified aerospace engineer with outstanding credentials and sound financial status, approached me about teaming up with me in some of my current activities. Rather than simply jumping at the opportunity, I allowed Matt to participate on a voluntary basis in several of our projects, and to tag along on numerous field exercises. After observing Matt carefully for approximately six months, I invited him to team up with me personally on a large multi-year project. Matt agreed to do so on the terms I proposed, with a small monthly salary to later be phased out in lieu of an incentive based program. He also agreed to relocate at his own personal cost. Matt's dedication has been exemplary and with his help in systematizing the highest payoff activities I'm currently engaged in, not only will my company realize tremendous profits, but Matt will also likely realize his dream of becoming a multimillionaire. In all discussions and in all written agreements with Matt, I have been very cautious and have been sure to only make commitments which are likely to be fulfilled by the company.

I have been in privately held organizations that I helped establish where others on the team simply were not willing to pull their own weight, and where they took advantage, perhaps without realizing it, of me and other team members. Furthermore, their habits were highly detrimental to the growth of the organization, and they had very little desire to change their ways. As a team leader, I remained somewhat blind to this, even though the signs were everywhere, and as a result I suffered delays in my own financial growth, as well as many other significant emotional pains. In another instance, I formed a company with three other people, two of whom were wrong for a startup organization. They weren't bad people, but they simply lacked the skills and personal commitment needed in such a venture. This alone cost the company approximately $50,000, much of which I personally funded, not to mention the many sleepless nights I experienced as a result.

Keep in mind that even people who have the right skills, desire, and attitude may not be right at a given point in time. They may have family issues, or financial constraints that make it difficult for them to endure the challenging environment of the typical fledgling venture. I speak from experience when I say, getting the right people on your team is essential to success.

In adding people to a team to help you employ time leverage, I suggest that you work and learn from knowledgeable entrepreneurs who personally understand the importance of leverage, systems, and having the right people onboard your team. Leverage their experience. Don't worry about the cost. It will more than pay for itself to get the right people on your team initially, and to avoid some of the mistakes most business owners make early in their entrepreneurial careers. With great people, you can realize great accomplishments, and can truly benefit from time leverage in ways you may not realize. With bad people, you may have significant heartache and may experience a very rough ride indeed.

Keep in mind that you can leverage the time of other people in ways that do not require building a team of people working under you, although that is where the greatest financial returns are usually realized. Likewise, you can accomplish significant gains by hiring others to do things for you that will free your time to focus on higher payoff activities. For example, unless you enjoy cutting the grass, hiring someone to perform this task while you focus on writing a book to publish on the Internet would be an excellent use of time leverage for financial gain, as well as the many other advantages you can realize from promoting your knowledge and ideas.

SWAPPING HOURS FOR DOLLARS

Let's examine this matter of "swapping hours for dollars" which I have mentioned several times in this book. This mentality is so widespread in America that the majority of our citizens, in one of the richest of all nations in terms of opportunity and wealth, are seemingly programmed that this is the only way to work.

Undoubtedly you have begun to have a few thoughts of your own regarding the leverage concept. If you truly realize the impact of the discussion in this section, you will go further toward unlocking your true potential than you might have ever dreamed.

Most individuals seem to be programmed to believe that swapping hours for dollars is the way to success, more particularly financial success. All of those who believe this are to some extent misled. Don't misunderstand me, you can live a fulfilling life without employing time leverage to any great extent, but you will never realize your full potential unless you get rid of this "swapping hours for dollars" mentality once and for all.

Consider Joe, the owner of a corner sandwich shop. He has developed a few outstanding recipes and has a solid flow of people passing through his store daily. He rarely spends any money advertising, because his clients spread the word for him. Joe makes a comfortable living and thoroughly enjoys running his sandwich shop. He longs to become wealthy, as do many of Joe's peers, but with the time he spends in the shop, there is little time to figure out how to do so. Joe has never seriously considered opening more than just the one shop of which he is so proud. Joe is your classic small business professional.

Jane on the other hand used to run a sandwich shop very much like Joe. In fact, Jane's original sandwich shop, on the other side of town, is still very similar to Joe's, and has a similar clientele and similar profit and loss statement. However, ten years ago Jane decided to create a system out of the things she had done well in building her reputable sandwich shop. She realized that the skills and product which had resulted in her shop being such a great success could be duplicated. So, she recorded the recipes and documented the procedures she followed, right down to the look of the advertising signs she used to announce specials in the window. She found several experienced businessmen willing to help her put it all together, and today she runs a highly profitable sandwich franchise. She has many stores throughout the United States that make the same great food, and they do it almost as well as she did. Yes, it took her quite a while to build the system, much of it in her spare time, but now instead of realizing a yearly profit of $50,000 Jane personally realizes a profit of well over $500,000. And she only works about 20 hours a week, because as things grew she built a team of highly qualified managers to run the show. Jane and Joe started at the same time, but Jane decided that she needed to find ways to take what she was doing and duplicate it through others, instead of simply swapping her hours for dollars.

Interestingly, today Jane is in the process of writing her autobiography, and she is also launching an online cookbook to teach others how to prepare some of the delicious sandwiches she has developed during her home experimentation. They'll be slightly different than those offered in her shops, but since Jane has learned how to unlock her mental potential, she has realized there is no limit to her creativity.

Let's look at another example of time leverage, this one from my own personal experience. I worked many years developing a broad base of skills ranging from technical skills to more communication intensive skills such as marketing, public speaking, and writing. Additionally, I chose to actively learn about and employ various forms of leverage vehicles useful in developing financial wealth, including real estate investing. Since before graduating from high school, my goal was to eventually begin teaching others the lessons I had learned through study and experience.

I began personal coaching, which I still do from time to time, for an hourly rate. Eventually I reached the point where I needed to branch out into teaching seminars in order to reach the amount of people with whom I desire to share what I've learned. Here I can teach 30 or more at one time the same things I might teach a student one on one. Whereas the student receiving private instruction might pay me $300 per hour for my time, I receive significantly more per hour for my time teaching in group sessions. This is an example of time leverage. I formed a team to support me in my efforts, freeing up my time so I can pursue more creative opportunities yielding greater returns on my effort. I leverage the time and talents of others.

After successfully spreading ideas in seminars I have begun developing audio programs which allow me to share on a much wider basis the winning ideas and strategies that have allowed me to realize many of my dreams. Experts in digital editing prepare the final audios and dedicated fulfillment centers create and ship the orders, all with little or no intervention on my part. I am now able to spread my ideas and strategies to many more people than I could ever reach in one on one consultations or in group settings. Not only are we promoting these products through our own company efforts, but we're also providing programs to affiliates with established marketing channels already in place. They receive a portion of the product sales dollars, and in turn we drastically increase our own revenues and overall profits. This is a true win-win situation and is another example of building a system to employ time leverage.

By employing leverage, we are not only able to offer more value to far more people than we might otherwise be able to do, but we are also able to increase our returns beyond what would otherwise be possible.

Ask yourself, "How can I leverage what I'm doing right now in a way that employs time leverage, or knowledge leverage, or some other form of leverage, so that my hours invested will produce far greater yields over time than if I simply invested my time in a totally non-leveraged fashion?"

As you begin thinking of how you spend your time, evaluate how to get more from the effort you spend than just the financial returns which that effort itself yields. If you cannot find a way, and you cannot find anyone to help you discover a way to leverage your time, then consider changing what you're doing.

Keep in mind that you may need to continue swapping hours for dollars in the short term.

Perhaps your current position, rather than being an end in and of itself needs to become a means to an end. Begin thinking of ways your current activities might be changed to lead you to a different outcome down the road. For example, I spent a good amount of time over the past half decade in one on one coaching, much of it without charge. During that time, I was considering how best to learn and perfect the message and information I was teaching, in preparation for one day launching the spread of my ideas and proven techniques across large quantities of people through a wide variety of vehicles. Therefore, although I was swapping hours for dollars in the short term, I was doing so with a larger objective; one that leverages time, rather than one that is time-linear in nature.

You only have so many hours in a day, and you have tremendous capabilities stored within you. There is a practically unlimited number of ways in which you can introduce leverage into what you're doing, so that you're not just swapping hours for dollars. You need to change your thinking along these lines or you will indeed end up achieving far less than you could otherwise achieve.

IT'S A MATTER OF SCALE

Let's look at the desire many of us have to achieve financial independence, usually meaning that we have developed sizable financial reserves in the form of performing assets -- assets that produce income with little direct effort.

First, realize that we live in a highly connected society. There are millions of people who can benefit from knowledge you personally possess or that you could easily possess if you sought to learn it. Likewise, if you are able to develop or deliver a product or service that has real value, and can do so just a little better than others in the market, the potential for outstanding success is remarkable.

With tremendous leverage vehicles like the Internet at your disposal, and with the hours available to most of us willing to take a little time to learn to think differently, the opportunities are practically endless. To realize significant financial returns, you simply have to find a way to deliver to a significant number of people something of enough value that you can realize a small amount of financial return for that idea, product, or service, from each person. For example, suppose you write a book that really sells well, eventually reaching 1,000,000 people over 10 years, with each person yielding 50 cents to you once all is said and done. You will have earned $500,000 for that work. If you did nothing else, that would be $50,000 per year. Yes, it may require a lot more than just writing a book to get that kind of return, but you get the picture. What if you have a product or service that can yield a $100 return per unit? How many people would you need to reach then? Do you see why learning to take advantage of leverage vehicles is so critical? Once you learn to employ leverage to reach enough people with a valuable service or product, becoming wealthy is no longer a question. It is only then a matter of time. Time leverage, coupled with knowledge leverage and diligent personal effort can produce results far beyond what many believe possible.

Think in terms of the scale necessary to achieve your goals and consider how you can employ leverage to help you reach those goals. Remember we are in a globally connected society and the ability you have today to reach a large number of people who might have a need for your product or service is greater than ever before. Carefully consider how time leverage fits into your success plan.

Think of a simple product or service you could create, which others would like or need. Consider how much you could sell this for, and then consider what leveraged methods you could employ for gradually increasing sales of this product or service until it generated enough income to make a difference in your life.

Chapter Three

Money Leverage

"If you cannot make money on one dollar, if you do not coax one dollar to work hard for you, you won't know how to make money out of one hundred thousand dollars."

— E. S. Kinnear

MONEY LEVERAGE

As an active real estate investor, this is one of my favorite topics. Money is a powerful tool for helping others, and since my life mission is to help as many people as I can during my brief stay in this world, I have sought and continue to seek ways to leverage money. The more I learn the more fun it becomes, and the wealthier I become in the process.

Let's begin with a simple example. Back in February, we took our annual trip to beautiful Hilton Head Island, SC. Just before leaving, a friend and I were discussing the concept of money leverage, and he said he needed a concrete example of how it might work. So, I said, "How about this. By the time I come back, a week or so from now, I'll make a few thousand dollars using none of my own money." He was quite skeptical.

As a part of my daily investing review, I had been tracking a stock that my ongoing research indicated was poised to grow substantially in the immediate future. Just before leaving, I placed an order for the stock, and since I would not be able to watch the stock's performance during my vacation, I issued a hard sell stop to protect my capital should my research and market timing prove inaccurate. The order was a margin order meaning I was using borrowed money for the purchase. When I returned, the stock had rocketed ahead by almost 50%. I sold the stock, pocketed nearly $5000, and called my friend. I would have normally held onto the stock, but I wanted to demonstrate my hobby of "minting money," a concept based on financial leverage.

This is a very simple example requiring specialized knowledge and correct market timing, and it carries a certain element of risk, but it is not at all unusual. Note also that this is not an example of a "day trade," although the time I held the stock was quite small. Market timing is difficult and if you wish to begin investing in securities, learn the ropes first, and consult with a carefully selected financial planner, preferably fee based to avoid conflicts of interest.

Let's look at another example. Late last year, Bryan approached me and advised he knew an older lady that owned a rental house which had been vacant for some time and was in need of repair. She wanted out of the rental business due to her age, and didn't really care what she received for the house. She told Bryan she'd sell for $17,000 in "as is" condition. My team and I evaluated the house and figured it would take approximately $5000 to repair. We worked with Bryan to purchase the property, legally structured the agreement so Bryan could make about $3000 in reselling it to us, and then found a private investor seeking a safe return on a secured investment to lend us the acquisition and fixup money. We left the closing with a check in our pocket, Bryan left the closing with check in his pocket, we fixed the house up for less than $5000, and we had an excellent rental property with no money out of pocket. Within just a couple of weeks we had the house rented with a positive cash flow of around $200 per month. The house appraised for $35,000. In summary, we obtained a performing asset with very little money out of pocket. This asset puts $200 cash in our pocket every month and if we chose to we could sell the asset and realize a healthy capital gain. This does not include the tax deferral we realize by offsetting normal income with the "paper" depreciation loss on the house. If we keep the property, over time the tenants will buy our house for us and we will own an asset free and clear that will continue to put money in our pocket every month. Taking advantage of time leverage, we hired an excellent property manager, and we have an office manager on staff that in turn manages our property manager.

Let's look at another example. We were approached by a group of family members that had inherited a neighborhood of rental homes and duplexes (two unit buildings) from their late parents. They did not want to be in the rental business and wanted to sell the properties to a company that could purchase the entire lot of properties. We found a reputable commercial lending organization that lent us almost the entire purchase price. The family then gave us money back to fix up the properties, and a private investor made up the difference, so that our financial investment was negligible. The properties were all occupied, are in an excellent area that is appreciating in value, and yield a solid monthly positive cash flow. On top of that, the properties appraised for over $250,000 more than the purchase price, and we've arranged to sell a good number of the properties at full retail to low income families for nothing down. The buyers' mortgage payments will be about what their rent is currently and they will enjoy the benefits of home ownership. We will sell these houses at fair market value, cash out about $100,000 of our equity, and keep the rest of the properties for future appreciation and cash flow.

While we're considering real estate examples, let's take a more general look at the powerful financial leverage real estate can offer, or more accurately, at the powerful financial leverage possible using real estate to secure money from others. When you offer real property as security for money from others, you can acquire much larger amounts of money and typically at much more attractive terms than would otherwise be available to you. And obtaining money on attractive terms when needed is critical to realizing the maximum benefit possible from the use of leverage.

It is not uncommon for the experienced investor to realize greater than 50% return on invested cash in the first year. Yes, it will certainly take a good while for the beginning investor to learn how to obtain this level of financial return from leveraged investments consistently, but once the experience is obtained, it is never lost. These are the incredible, wealth producing returns that are possible when you learn to properly employ money leverage.

Seek out a local real estate investment club, find out who the experienced real estate investors are in the area, and invite them to lunch, one by one, to learn how you might begin investing in real estate. Don't get pulled in by the get-rich-quick courses. Realize that almost all successful real estate investors got started slowly and took the long-term view of real estate as an investment vehicle.

So how do you, the average person, begin really benefiting from situations such as these? First, you must gain financial intelligence. Money has rules, and you must understand those rules. You must understand the vocabulary, you must develop sound personal financial habits, and you must learn how the money game is played. Trying to participate in activities like real estate where there is high financial leverage, without sound financial habits and a clear understanding of the business and rules of money, is not recommended. Attend seminars, read books, and listen to educational audio programs to enhance your knowledge of the rules of money as well as the financial leverage vehicle you wish to employ, *before* risking your own financial reserves. Study sound money management principles. Learn about the basics of stocks, bonds, and other financial vehicles.

Learn about real estate investing. Consider hiring knowledgeable experts to assist you in your initial live efforts.

How many books and audio programs do you have in your personal library that you study from time to time? How often do you study financial matters and investing? How many seminars do you attend each year to help you find creative ways to grow and invest your assets? If you have not already done so, write down a plan of action and begin expanding your financial knowledge today! If you're not continually expanding your financial knowledge, your ability to realize significant long-term wealth is weak. Once you fully understand the basics and have a sound financial foundation, you'll be in a position to take advantage of the many leveraged financial vehicles which can lead you quickly to new financial heights.

Once you begin to look for ways to leverage money, and you begin to understand how money works, you will begin to notice opportunities. Explore these, and learn from as many real life examples as possible. Remember, don't do what the average person is doing. Rather, seek out people who are wealthy or who are clearly well on their way to being wealthy, and learn what they're doing. How do they make their money work for them? You're far better learning from someone who has arrived at, or is going where you want to go, than someone who has simply dreamed of going where you want to go but has never made the first step on the journey.

RETURN ON INVESTMENT

One of the most fundamental concepts that absolutely must be understood if you are to measure the effectiveness of the financial leverage employed in your investment activities, and the overall positive growth of your assets, is the concept of Return on Investment, or ROI. Indeed, most wealthy people regularly use this measurement to evaluate performance of their various investments.

ROI is the return, generally in percentage points, that a given investment yields over a specified time frame. Most investment yields, as well as most loan rates, are given in yearly figures. This is likely the most suitable timeframe over which to consider your investment yields.

For example, let's assume you invest $10,000 of your own money in a particular investment. If this investment provides $1000 in profit in one year then your ROI is $1000 / $10,000 or

10%. The higher the yield the faster your money is working for you and the faster your wealth will grow.

Let's figure the ROI for one of the examples listed earlier in this chapter. In the example of the house we picked up from the lady referred to us by Bryan, we initially invested none of our own cash, using 100% borrowed funds for the acquisition. In fact, we left the closing with approximately $3000 in our pocket. After closing, we spent about $5000 repairing the property and getting it rented. After it was rented, it yielded $200 per month in positive cash flow. Neglecting the fact that the tenant was actually repaying part of our debt on the property in addition to the positive cash flow we received, and neglecting the fact that we received appreciation on the property over time, we realized a positive profit from rents of about $200 x 12 = $2400 per year. Our net initial investment out of pocket was approximately $2000 ($5000 repairs minus $3000 loan proceeds received at closing). So our average ROI the first year, neglecting appreciation, debt repay, and tax benefits from depreciation, was $2400 / $2000 = 120%. This rate of return sure beats the rates people realize from traditional non-leveraged investments!

Remember that we picked up approximately $10,000 in equity on the day of closing. If we sold the property we would be able to convert a good bit of this equity into cash. However, by keeping it as equity in the property, we defer the tax liabilities we'd realize from converting the asset to cash. If you factored in the first year growth in our net worth due to the initial equity into the ROI equation, the overall yield would be much higher. In fact, if you look at the overall profits from all aspects of this real estate investment, which includes the capital gains realized through acquiring the real estate at below market prices, as well as the various profit centers associated with real estate investing, the overall ROI in this example is much higher than that noted above.

Our companies average, on an annual basis, an overall return of well over 30% per year on our investments, all forms of gain considered. This rate of return is not at all unusual in real estate investment companies that truly understand the business, and the proper application of money leverage. This explains why real estate is perhaps one of the most popular leveraged investment vehicles of all time.

What annual rate of return are you receiving from your investments? If it is not at least 10%, consider what leveraged investment vehicle you might be able to employ, beginning with a small investment, to expand your options for higher and faster growth of your assets. Set aside a small amount of money, and actually invest this money in the vehicle of your choice, being careful to learn as much as you can about the vehicle, and ensuring that at least some steps are in place to ensure you will not lose your principal investment. Experience is a great teacher, just remember to start small.

PRIVATE LENDING FOR HIGH ROI

There are many ways to realize very high yields on relatively safe investments, if you have specialized knowledge. Let me share with you another way that I am able to keep my money growing at my personal benchmark of 30% per year minimum yield.

As I love real estate investments, I have become well connected in the real estate community. Since the way to create very high yields in real estate is to buy at a deep discount, and then leverage the investment highly based on the purchase price, ready access to other people's money is required. One of my primary strategies for obtaining money for deals is to use small commercial banks for primary financing, and then to use private investors to make up the difference. After a short hold time of six to nine months, I typically either sell the investment at market value, cashing out the gains or rolling them into another investment using a tax free exchange, or I refinance the investment with a larger bank as part of a bundled portfolio of properties, realizing a refinanced loan amount equal to or exceeding the sum of the loans used during my initial investment purchase. Indeed, often I am not only able to pay off my original loans, but am able to also pocket a small amount of excess loan proceeds to use as additional investment capital. Since I buy property this way, I show other investors how to buy property this way as well. Then when they need money, I use funds I've saved in various financial investment accounts to lend to them on terms that make their investment work, giving them the high short term yields they require. In return I realize a yield of approximately 30% on my investment.

For example, I will loan money, usually in amounts ranging from $25,000 to $75,000, charging 2 to 4 percent up front for the money with an annual interest rate of 12% to 18%, having interest only payments due monthly. Generally, I require the borrower to pledge collateral in the form of attractive real estate with positive equity after all loans on the property are considered. This way if the borrower cannot honor the loan agreement, I will be able to pick up another attractive investment for my real estate portfolio and will not lose the financial investment.

To explain the effective ROI realized from this type of investment, let's consider a specific example. Suppose I loan $25,000 to an investor for three months, and I charge the investor 3 points (3 percent) up front for the privilege of borrowing the funds and an annual interest rate of 15%. This is a realistic example of various investments I've made over the past year. Let's calculate the equivalent annual yield.

Investment: $25,000, 3 points, 15% annual interest rate

Up front profit: $25,000 x 3% = $750

Monthly interest: $25,000 x 15% / 12 = $312.50

Interest over 3 months: $312.50 x 3 = $937.50

Total profit over 3 months: $750 + $937.50 = $1687.50

Annualized return: $1687.50 x 12 / 3 = $6750

Equivalent annual rate of return: $6750 / $25,000 = 27%

Keep in mind that as soon as one investment cashes out, I need to get the money invested again quickly if I am to realize the overall annual yield, but to date this has not been a problem as there are always people needing money and once you have some investment capital you simply need to ensure you invest it wisely.

To further boost yields on my investments, I use investment funds in retirement accounts with a non-traditional custodian that allows private investments such as the one outlined above. Therefore, depending on the type of account, my returns are either tax deferred or tax free, and thus my capital grows much faster than it would if I had to take out proceeds to cover income taxes on the earnings. This vastly increases the yields I receive over time and essentially increases the time leverage employed in the growth of my assets.

The above example of private lending is another example of leverage in action, except in this case, I'm helping investors see how to make their leveraged investments work using my money in a fashion that gives me high returns on my investment capital. Why do I invest capital in this manner instead of investing all of my capital in real estate directly? Simply, its a matter of time. This type of investment provides a relatively high yield with controlled risk, but requires much less time than does a real estate investment using the same amount of capital. In fact, this is only one of numerous ways that I employ assets in vehicles that at some point involve leverage to generate excellent returns.

COMPOUND INTEREST

To truly understand the power of having a high rate of return, coupled with time, let's consider now what may be one of the greatest discoveries in history, compound interest. You've no doubt heard about it, and you've likely learned about it and been counseled to put it to use, but if you're like most people, you don't give serious thought to the tremendous leverage this one vehicle offers.

Compound interest is perhaps one of the most exciting leverage concepts known to man. When you combine wealth producing rates of return with just a few decades of time, the results can be staggering. Let's consider a few examples. Suppose you start a real estate investing business to build an investment portfolio of real estate properties. After a few challenging years, where patience and persistence are greatly employed, you finally reach a point of profitability. You're realizing a healthy 30% return on your invested capital per year. Each year you're able to compound that return by reinvesting the capital generated by your portfolio. Assume that you begin with $10,000 that you generated using "nothing down" real estate techniques. You basically "minted" the first $10,000 in investment capital. Over a period of 25 years, you will have realized a total growth in your portfolio of over $7,000,000. Yes, that's over seven million dollars! That's the power of compound interest. If this seems unbelievable then consider how many of the relatively young billionaires in our country would view this amount. Remember, if you shoot for the stars, you're a lot less likely to end up in the mud.

If you haven't done so, go to the Internet and use one of the popular search engines such as Google™ (www.google.com) to search for the compound interest formula (search for "compound interest calculator" or "future value calculator"). You'll find numerous sites where you can use this formula to run your own projections. If you don't know how to search the Internet or don't have a computer, find out how and find a computer. There are many places where you can access computers for free, like your local library.

The trick is to learn what you need to know to realize this type of return. There are many resources out there to help you, if you'll just take the time and make the effort to find them. Learn how to put this tremendous tool of compound interest to work for you today.

Keep in mind, the earlier you begin investing to realize the power of compound interest the better. I am amazed at the number of teenagers that spend every penny they can beg, borrow, and earn on the latest clothes or car fashion of the day, striving to fit in with their peers. If they'd only take a portion of those proceeds, learn early on how to invest it wisely, with wealth producing rates of return, they'd realize in their lifetime far greater wealth than most ever see. Don't make the same mistake. Begin today investing for your future.

COMBINING FORMS OF LEVERAGE

Now that we've examined two forms of leverage, let's consider another principle that you must consider as you apply leverage in your life. As we have discussed, time leverage and money leverage are incredibly powerful leverage tools. However, as successful people familiar with the concept of leverage will tell you, when you combine leverage vehicles, the rewards are far greater than simply a twofold increase. It is more like rewards squared, just as 5 plus 5 is 10 but five squared is 25. So, as we discuss money leverage examples, consider how these might be combined with the power of time and knowledge leverage. In fact, when considering any type of leverage opportunity, think carefully about all the types of leverage that might be applicable to the particular situation.

Consider your age and savings. Assume you want to retire at some point, and have your assets produce income sufficient to fund your desired standard of living in retirement at a rate of 8%, a rate which can be realized from relatively safe investments. Let's assume that inflation will eat up 3% of the yields, so that your net effective return over time is only 5% if you have an overall rate of 8% on the final investment portfolio. Figure how much you'll need to invest today, and at what ROI, to build the portfolio you need at retirement. To calculate this amount, go to www.google.com on the internet and search for "future value formula." Play with the numbers. It is an eye opening experience.

For example:

Let's assume you want to have $25,000 yearly income at retirement. You therefore need, assuming a net yield of 5% at that time on your portfolio, an amount equal to:

$25,000 / 0.05 = $500,000

Assume you have $10,000 at this time to invest, and you want to retire in 20 years. Using the future value calculator you found on the Internet, you input the following values:

Principal: $10,000
Years: 20
Future value: $500,000

You find that the rate of return you must have today on your investments is 21.6%. If you have less time, and the same principal, the rate would have to be even higher! It is important to be realistic about your plans, so do this exercise today!

Chapter Four

Knowledge Leverage

"In the information age, knowledge is the ultimate power. The fastest way to tap into this power is to leverage the knowledge of others."

— Ron D. Pate

KNOWLEDGE LEVERAGE

Today there is far more information available than any one individual could ever possibly assimilate in a normal lifetime. To achieve the highest levels of success, more knowledge typically needs to be employed than any one individual can likely acquire on his or her own. This trend is increasing as we enter further into the Information Age. Therefore, it is essential to develop relationships and build a network of competent people around you that supplement your own knowledge, so that you can leverage their knowledge to advance you on your journey of success.

To employ knowledge leverage to the maximum extent possible, and with the most effectiveness possible, it is essential that you develop a good set of knowledge skills yourself. You must possess a sufficient amount of knowledge to understand and engage in meaningful communication with other people, and to interpret and apply the knowledge that you gain from them. If you wish to go far in life, achieving greater financial success than those around you, it is essential to dedicate yourself to lifelong learning. Perhaps one of the best ways to learn, and to position yourself to take maximum advantage of knowledge leverage opportunities, is to find a few competent mentors to guide you on your journey.

MENTORS

You should constantly be on the lookout for successful people. As you find them, consider how you can learn what they did to become successful and how you can model their actions and behaviors. Much can be learned through passive observation, but to truly gain the insights you need, you must establish a relationship with the successful person. Interestingly enough, successful people are usually willing to help those who truly want to be helped. For example, as a local real estate expert, I regularly allow new real estate investors to take me to lunch, at which time I share some of my insights while learning about the challenges they are facing. I have also had numerous occasions where I was at a seminar or with someone having an outstanding track record, and I shared a cup of coffee at break, or in the hallway, asking pertinent questions and usually obtaining golden nuggets of powerful insight.

Having knowledgeable mentors from whom you learn on a regular basis is perhaps one of the most powerful ways to position yourself to employ knowledge leverage that you will find. Mentors come in many varieties, and whether you are mentored for 15 minutes or you have an ongoing relationship wherein you are guided by your mentor weekly, you're gaining valuable insights, often at little or no cost.

Keep in mind mentors don't have to be in person. Zig Ziglar, Earl Nightingale, Denis Waitley, and Tony Robbins are all mentors that I listen to or read regularly, even though I do not regularly spend time with them in person.

It cannot be stressed enough. If you truly want to reach the heights of success, you do not have time to reinvent the wheel. The factors that lead to success are time proven, and readily available to you. You simply have to seek them out. Seeking out competent mentors, both in person and through educational materials is absolutely critical. If you do nothing more than study over and over again, and most importantly, apply the concepts in this book, as well as the many other success reference materials available to you today, then you will truly create remarkable life changes in the years to come. It doesn't happen overnight, as some late night infomercials would have you believe, but it does happen. Once you program yourself for success, it is simply amazing what begins to happen. Make sure leverage is in your success tool kit.

Find out who the most respected and knowledgeable person is in a field that you consider important to your future success. Buy and study this expert's books or audios, or better yet, attend a live event where this person will be speaking. Try to meet this expert and learn from his or her experience. Leverage the knowledge of others to allow you to progress on your journey of success at a more rapid pace!

BUILDING A TEAM

In the section on Time Leverage we discussed building a team as a way to realize leverage of the time of others. Building a team is perhaps even more important when it comes to leveraging the knowledge of others. Many people lose time, and often lose significant percentages of their available money, when they fail to realize the importance of leveraging the knowledge of others through a team of advisors, affiliates, or employees.

If you study the wealthy of our society, you'll realize that they rely heavily on expert advice, and they pay handsomely for such advice. The truly successful realize that to develop the knowledge themselves which is required for outstanding success would require a prohibitive amount of time. Therefore, they seek the knowledge of others more competent than themselves in critical areas. Often this is in the form of mentors, or professional advisors. These include financial advisors, relationship advisors, business advisors, investment and life coaches, accounting advisors, and so on. Indeed, when I'm teaching entrepreneur or real estate investing success strategies, one of the first things I will point out to the budding entrepreneur or investor is the need for a team of advisors.

I regularly study the lives and examples of highly successful people. There is an interesting story about Henry Ford, a highly successful businessman and entrepreneur. During an interview, a reporter trying to show that Mr. Ford was not very intelligent kept asking him technical questions. When Mr. Ford couldn't answer the questions the reporter started to heckle him about his lack of knowledge. Mr. Ford responded by calling and asking one of his employees the question. After another question he did the very same thing.

Then he turned to the reporter and said. "I don't need to know all of the answers to run a successful company. I have hired people to answer these questions for me so I can concentrate on steering the ship."

This story points out a simple but profound concept that so many miss. It is not important that you know every little detail about a given important topic, but rather that you understand the power of knowledge leverage, and that you know where to find the answer. This also offers clues into the power of having a team at your disposal to supplement your own knowledge.

Most entrepreneurs realize that a team of third party advisors is not enough to achieve the maximum growth and success possible. Instead, it is important to build a team under you, and around you, to supplement your knowledge, as well as your time. Most highly successful people do their best to surround themselves with people even smarter than they themselves are.

When a team is developed in the right way, with a win-win spirit coupled with a passionate mission that the team can grab onto, everyone in the team reaps the rewards of knowledge leverage. Indeed, a team of three of the right individuals will accomplish far more than three individuals on their own could ever hope to accomplish. If one of the individuals, or the team originator, has high morals and values, and inspires the team in the right way, the results can be truly outstanding. Developing a powerful, inspired team can be one of the most rewarding ways to use time and knowledge leverage that you might ever experience.

THE INTERNET

As has been mentioned before, the Internet brings to our fingertips a vehicle that can allow you to leverage the knowledge of others in ways unimagined in previous centuries. Even though the growth of the Internet, and the influence it is having on our way of life, is just beginning, it is already perhaps the most incredible knowledge distribution vehicle ever conceived. I can say without a doubt that the knowledge and time leverage the Internet offers could make you wealthy beyond your wildest dreams if you truly understood sound business principles and if you studied and diligently learned how to leverage its power.

The root source of the leverage of the Internet is closely related to the concept of networking. Perhaps it will be helpful to illustrate the power of this concept by using an example which is familiar to all of us -- your own brain. Even with all the modern advances in computer technology, the power of computers still lags significantly behind the power of the human brain. The reason the brain is so powerful is the way it is designed. Your brain has a staggering amount of neural interconnections. It is precisely these interconnections that allow such a small organ to produce such unbelievable results. To truly realize how incredible the amount of interconnections in your brain are consider the following. An atom is one of the smallest particles known to man. It has been estimated that the total amount of atoms in the known universe is, when written as a number, on the order of 10 with one hundred 0's behind it. In comparison, the estimated number of interconnections and patterns the neurons in the average human brain can make may be as many as 10 with eight hundred 0's after it! *

As more and more knowledge is added to the Internet, as the speed and availability of access to that knowledge increases, and as the

---

* Tony Buzcan, *Use Both Sides of Your Brain* (New York: E.P. Dutton, 1976), pg.17

tools on the Internet that allow you to leverage that knowledge increase, the possibilities for outstanding results to be produced from the use of the Internet also increase. The amount of interconnections on the Internet is increasing at lightning speed, and hence the power of this network is also increasing at a tremendous rate.

If you are not considering ways to employ the knowledge leverage the Internet offers you in your own personal life, or in your career or business, you should do so without hesitation. Learn, study, and use this powerful knowledge leverage tool.

SHARPEN THE SAW

The term "leverage" arises from the word "lever" which is the tool on which physical leverage is based. Indeed, as noted earlier, thousands of years ago Archimedes coined the phrase, "Give me a lever and I can move the world."

In order to realize the maximum leverage possible, the tool must be in good shape. Just as outlined before, if your tool is a team, you must have the right members on it. If you're using a physical lever to move a heavy object, the physical lever needs to be strong. Likewise, if you wish to employ knowledge leverage to the maximum extent possible, your tools must be well developed. And your most important tool is your own brain.

As success authority Stephen Covey has so aptly pointed out, it is critical that you continuously "sharpen your saw." Your saw, or tool, in this case is your own knowledge. It is also widely quoted that "leaders are readers." In fact, the statistical evidence clearly indicates that those who read and study on a regular basis are indeed the successful of our society, and in general the most healthy and wealthy of our generation, as well as previous generations.

Therefore, if you wish to achieve the maximum success possible in your own life, and if you wish to employ knowledge leverage to the maximum extent possible, you yourself must develop the consistent habit of feeding your brain quality, carefully chosen information designed to enhance your overall knowledge. This knowledge should cover general success principles, life balance, career and business, and all other important areas of your life.

It is very important that you carefully choose what you expose your mind to. Unlike your conscious mind, your subconscious, which significantly impacts what you become, does not distinguish between good and bad. It takes in whatever you give it. Just as you would not put water in your automobile's gas tank, give your mind the fuel that it needs for maximum success.

With the right focus and diligent application, leverage of your own knowledge and more importantly the knowledge of others, can move you forward on your personal journey of success faster than you might have ever imagined.

KNOWLEDGE LEVERAGE IN ACTION

Let's look at a few simple examples of knowledge leverage in action. In helping others, I obtained a few clients that I used to assist with various types of coaching. One of our clients located an attractive real estate investment opportunity. This was his first investment property. As I understand a variety of ways bank financing can be creatively used to increase the yields on real estate investments, Don asked me to assist him in developing the best strategy for financing this first investment. I referred Don to a lender who understood and had a product to support this type of transaction. Additionally, I suggested how he might approach and finance this property's purchase, and explained to him the risks, rewards, and technical aspects of implementing this financing methodology. As a result, Don was able to buy a house worth $164,000 for approximately $145,000, and receive almost 100% financing at an interest rate well under 4%. This allowed him to acquire a property with very little money out of pocket that yielded a positive cash flow of over $500 per month. His return on invested capital was extremely high and the fact that he had a good measure of equity in the property, which is in an appreciating neighborhood, additionally protected him from interest rate risk. As Don had never purchased a real estate investment property before, if he attempted to figure out the optimum financing strategy and to seek the right lender to provide financing on this particular property, it is highly unlikely he would have received anywhere near the terms he was able to obtain in this case. Don leveraged my knowledge, which in turn saved him thousands of dollars and resulted in his receiving a significantly higher return on investment than he would have otherwise realized.

Let's look at another simple example of knowledge leverage. As I am interested in using all available vehicles for distributing the success information I have gathered and teach, I knew I needed to write this book, as well as several others that are in process. I also knew that I had very little understanding of the publishing industry. Rather than try to figure it out on my own, I contacted a friend active in this industry for many years. I asked James if he could help me learn what I needed to know in order to realize my dream of becoming a published author, allowing me to share my knowledge and experience with others through well written books. He helped me understand within a matter of hours critical things that an aspiring author must take into account, as well as many additional interesting insights that led to this very book you now hold. Had I tried to figure all this out on my own, I may never have realized my dream of having these ideas published for the world to read. I leveraged, and continue to leverage, James' knowledge.

Examples of knowledge leverage abound, and opportunities to leverage the knowledge of others exist in every aspect of your life. Seek these opportunities, and realize that your own capacity for mental growth is indeed unlimited.

How many hours per day do you spend "sharpening your saw?" Make it a habit to read an educational book or to use the Internet at least a few minutes each day to enhance your knowledge of critical matters such as financial intelligence.

Let's close out this chapter with another example of knowledge leverage. I employ numerous investment methodologies and strategies in real estate investing. One of my favorites is to find an old, physically deteriorated building that still has the potential to be rehabilitated, and to bring that building back to life. Indeed there are many investors that "rehab" houses as their main line of work. Many "rehabbers" do most of the work themselves, only calling in specialists for activities that require licensed professionals, such as installing new wiring and plumbing. I on the other hand take a different approach. Rather than try to do the work myself, I hire other contractors to perform the reconstruction activities. It is true that I do this in order to leverage their time, as my time is more valuable finding, negotiating, and buying the property than it is in performing the repairs. However, there is an even more important reason why I utilize other parties to perform this work. I want to leverage their knowledge. An experienced contractor who rebuilds property as a profession is much more likely to perform this job effectively and efficiently than someone who only engages in the repair as one of many other activities. In other words, I leverage the knowledge and experience of the professionals instead of myself trying to do it all. This is another excellent example of combining two forms of leverage together, in this case time and knowledge leverage.

Chapter Five

Wealth Concepts

"Financial wealth is elusive only to those who do not understand the wealthy mindset and who have not learned the rules of the money game."

— Ron D. Pate

WEALTH CONCEPTS

One of the primary reasons people learn to employ leverage is to realize a level of wealth in their active lifetime which will afford them the financial freedom to explore all that life has to offer, without the burden of financial constraints. If this is your goal, or if realizing powerful financial results in your life is important to you, it is important to understand various fundamentals about wealth.

Over the years, I've studied a tremendous amount of materials on success and wealth, have spoken with many highly successful individuals in a wide variety of disciplines, and through my own experience have learned what I consider to be some of the most important factors in wealth creation. Many of these are inherently built upon a foundation of leverage. If you truly learn each of these, and apply what you learn, you will realize financial rewards you might have previously considered impossible.

Before we examine these ideas of wealth, let's agree on one thing. Money is good. It is the misuse of money that is bad. The trade of services and goods is a vital part of what makes a society work, and money is the trade vehicle of choice in most modern countries. The more service and value you provide to others, the more money you will typically receive. I have heard many people use the Bible to classify money as evil. The Bible does not read "money is the root of all evil." It reads, "the love of money is the root of all evil" (1 Timothy 6:10). That is a totally different meaning. There is an accurate saying that "money makes a bad person worse and a good person better." A great deal of money in the hands of a person with significant character flaws may indeed lead to undesirable consequences. But in the hands of a person having strong positive values, outstanding character, and a good measure of self-control, money can be a tool used to accomplish a great deal of good in the community, and in the lives of others. Money is just like any other tool. It can be used for good, or it can be used for bad. Over the years, I have dined with numerous wealthy individuals. These accomplished individuals are generally the healthiest, have the best disposition, and give back to society much more than the average individual. Indeed, the reason they typically have so much is because they have become the type of people who deserve a great deal, usually through their giving greatly in terms of service to society, whether through their companies, or their individual efforts.

As has been said by several successful individuals, "I've been poor and I've been wealthy, and I'd take wealthy any day." Don't let the people around you who have achieved little in the way of financial rewards in their life try to convince you they're glad they didn't achieve more. They may tell you, "I don't want to be financially independent." Keep in mind, this is often just self-talk to help them deal with their own personal frustrations or regrets. Having money, with the proper respect for the things it will offer you, is the power to do good and the power to give to others, to help others in need, and to provide the best care possible to yourself and your family. No, money is not a necessity for a happy or fulfilling life, but it can greatly enhance your life, and the lives of those around you, if used properly.

I remember one day I was speaking with Ann, a friend of my family, and she shared with me how she had fallen on hard times. On the spot I offered to lend her $10,000 that she could pay back when things improved. And then another time I sent a $1000 money order anonymously to a friend in need. The joy I received from helping friends in this way, and seeing the way it changed their lives for the better, is priceless. That's the power of money when it is properly applied.

> What are your feelings regarding money? How would your life be different if you had plenty of money at your disposal for anything you could dream of? What would you do with your money? How would you behave differently? How would you help others?

FINANCIAL INDEPENDENCE

Many people I meet say they dream of the day when they are financially independent. Curiously many of these same individuals have no concrete understanding of what this truly means. Personally, I consider financial independence as possessing enough performing assets to produce, without your own personal time contribution, a sufficient financial return for you to live the life you have designed for yourself and your family. Once you reach this point in life, you are free to do the things in life that you truly wish to do, to focus on and fulfill your life purpose, without difficult financial constraints. Keep in mind that accumulating abundant financial wealth is <u>not</u> a recommended life purpose. Money should be the result of a life well lived, not the other way around. Financial wealth is a tool to help you accomplish your life purpose, but it is not itself your life purpose. Interestingly, those who become financially independent generally never waste the time they receive from having this independence, and usually they continually build assets and additional cash flow through their actions even though they may not be focused specifically on that goal. Financial reward is generally a reflection of your service to others, and it is greatly enhanced by and through the leverage vehicles you employ to achieve success.

Let's look at an example. Suppose you have 100 residential rental units yielding a positive cash flow of $100 per unit per month, or $10,000 per month in net profits. Rents are generally increasing from year to year and your tenants are paying down your debt so that over time this stream of passive income increases much greater than inflation, meaning you truly have more and more money each month. You also have over the past several years learned to successfully invest in stocks, and through focused effort have developed a portfolio where you, with the advice of your fee based financial adviser, trade enough to generate another $3000 per month average in cash, while your long-term portfolio yields growth in capital appreciation over a longer timeframe.

You spend a few hours a week managing your portfolio. In addition, you have published a book, both in hardcopy and e-book format that brings in around $2000 per month from your website, local bookstores, and targeted resellers. Finally, over the past ten years, you developed a very successful graphics design firm, which you sold with residual income arrangements that provide you with another $5,000 per month in income. You have a monthly income of $20,000 with no more than 20 to 30 hours per week invested. Your standard of living calls for about $10,000 per month, so even if you stopped the active efforts you are making to earn money and hired out someone to cover for you on those matters, you would still exceed your financial requirements. Of course, you take the additional $10,000 per month you're realizing and reinvest it, further increasing your security. You are, by my definition as noted earlier, financially independent.

Note that the above example includes a good amount of passive income from sources that require little personal attention to generate the cash flow stream. The need for only minimal personal time commitment is a critical consideration if you wish to grow large quantities of passive income.

Is financial independence one of your goals? If so, how do you define financial independence? What level of income producing assets would you need to become financially independent? To determine this may require the assistance of a professional financial planner, but if so, it's well worth it to know this target. Make sure you know exactly what your long-term financial goals are and keep them in front of you at all times to drive you toward your dreams.

THE WEALTH MENTALITY

Individuals who become very wealthy seem to have a different way of thinking than the average individual. They have a "wealthy mindset." Just as it is necessary to develop a success mentality to succeed in life, it is necessary to develop a wealth mentality to become wealthy. This is one of the most critical steps you must take if you wish to become financially independent.

To develop a wealth mentality, you may need to eliminate or adjust a lot of ideas and beliefs that you have obtained from your family, friends, or associates. Most likely, you're going to catch some heat from those you love most. But to whom would you rather listen for financial advice, someone who is not financially successful, or someone who is financially independent and that has rapidly growing financial resources?

One of the mental visualizations I enjoy practicing is to imagine myself lying on the ground looking up at the sky, seeing the trillions of dollars that flow through our economy every day passing overhead. It's a steady stream of money. All I have to do is to find a way to dip into this stream and pull out a tiny portion of the stream in order to have all the financial resources I need. Having an abundance mentality is one of the most important first steps to developing a wealthy mindset. If you are to achieve wealth, you must believe you can achieve it and this means throwing out the scarcity mentality once and for all.

Let's take a look at some of the ideas and notions you may have that need to be modified. By evaluating what not to believe or do, you will more clearly see the attitudes and beliefs that you must develop.

Practice visualizing the huge amount of money that passes through our economic system every day. Imagine yourself tapping into this steady stream of money and pulling just a small stream to yourself. Money is not in any way scarce, but you must believe you can attract money and you must learn techniques to do so. Visualizing and believing you can do so is the first step to making it a reality.

EMPLOYMENT LEVERAGE

Perhaps one of the most obvious distinctions between the majority of the very wealthy and the rest of society is the perception of a job. All during your life, you've likely heard, "Go to college, work hard, and get good grades so that you can get a good job." But in the context of leverage, and considering many of the jobs available, where you're working for someone else swapping hours for dollars, just how much leverage are you employing? You are employing no leverage, or at best very little. If your goal is to become wealthy, a job working for someone else may need to be viewed as a temporary inconvenience. Rather than a lifelong engagement, your job might be just a vehicle through which you gain experience in certain areas, such as teamwork, and a way of generating cash flow to cover your daily living expenses while you study and learn from the sidelines and set up your leverage vehicles. It is true that not all individuals are cut out to be entrepreneurs, but most have friends or associates that are entrepreneurs, and there are ways to remove the financial achievement caps as a team that minimize the risks of going it alone. It is an established and well recognized fact that relatively few of the very wealthy of our society achieved their wealth by working for someone else in linear fashion.

Think back to the examples I've already shared with you, and consider others as you read ahead. On which side of the employer/employee relationship does the leverage opportunity exist?

To better understand this concept, consider one definition of the ideal employee. The ideal employee is one who generates significantly more value for the organization than that individual receives from the organization as compensation, all types of compensation included. Think about how a company grows and increases profits. Where does the growth originate? Usually it originates in the minds and actions of the team members who work for the organization. So, where do the excess profits the organization realizes ultimately originate? The profits originate with the employees. You see the organization, if it is properly structured for growth, is leveraging the intelligence and time of the team members it employs. What happens when economic factors, or other factors, change the equation such that the excess employee value realized by the organization is less than the value needed by the organization to survive and grow?

Usually the organization takes measures to reduce costs, often including removing employees providing the least value, and replacing them with more productive employees, or automated systems, in order to improve profitability.

You see, if you are an employee, you are one of the leverage tools used by the organization and those running the organization. If you are the employer, or the head of the organization which you individually or with others create, then you are leveraging those who work for you, the employees. It goes back to the basics of time and knowledge leverage.

RESIDUAL INCOME

Perhaps the ultimate wealth creation strategy, the ultimate use of leverage, is to create automatic residual streams of income. These income streams, generated by performing assets that produce profits without significant active management, provide cash flow to you whether you work or not. Some of the more popular residual income sources that produce wealth producing rates of return include active real estate investments managed by professional property managers, private loans and business investments, brick and mortar businesses that are built up and turned over to competent management for daily oversight, and Internet based businesses specializing in information based product distribution. As you begin your wealth development journey, learn as much about the concept of residual income as possible. Remember, with regard to leverage, most successful residual income opportunities consist of numerous leverage vehicles rolled into one.

Whenever I approach a business opportunity I always look at it from every angle possible to see what different models I can develop that will offer me the ability to walk away from the daily management of the opportunity while receiving a good financial return on my investment of time and other resources, over and over again. I try to find ways to use the opportunity to generate residual streams of income, streams that will produce plentiful cash flow with minimal oversight. Keep in mind that, from a financial perspective, cash flow is what, in most cases, has the largest impact on your quality of life. And, performing assets are the source of residual cash flow, the source of your residual streams of income.

The ability to create residual streams of income has never been greater than it is today, primarily because of the explosion of information and its use.

Let's consider an example. Suppose I develop a dynamic idea that will, almost certainly, save a local company substantial amounts of money. I contact the head of the organization, which has annual sales in excess of $100,000,000, and explain my idea which is based on information discovered through appropriate research. Instead of an up front fee to share this idea, all I want is for the company to agree to pay me 25% of the savings, once they are realized. If they save nothing, they owe nothing, if they save a significant amount, then they keep 75% of the savings that they likely wouldn't have realized without my idea. After obtaining the proper legal agreements protecting my rights, I share the idea, explaining how the company might begin its implementation. The savings are approximately $100,000 per year. My share is $25,000 per year, for five years. That's not a bad return on one idea. Assuming the company is viable and remains in business during the term of our agreement, I have created a residual income stream with a five year life.

Think of the other cash flow streams you have read and will read about throughout this book. Consider how you might develop some residual income streams of your own. Do you have a tangible skill of some sort that could be utilized to create a product or service which could be sold over and over again without your direct effort every time? If not, what interests you enough that you might learn in your spare time how to create such a product or service?

As you continue to learn more and more about personal and business success principles, your own ideas will begin to flow. Be sure to take action on those ideas, and before you know it you will have developed your first source of residual income, and then you will truly be on your way.

SECURITY

Ask most people why they work for someone else, and they may say it's for security. Most people never consider any way to earn a living other than working for someone else, even though they never realize any substantial measure of financial accomplishment. Based on personal experience, as well as many conversations with highly successful individuals, I am convinced there is no real security in working for someone else as a typical hourly or salary based employee. In fact, I'd go so far as to say that employment security is an illusion. There is no real security, only differing degrees of risk.

The search for security may even be a little dangerous, especially to your financial future, and possibly to your ability to realize your dreams as well. The more you look for and strive for security, the more you will avoid risk. If you avoid risk, you likely avoid opportunity, and avoiding opportunity carries a very high price indeed, the price of success. You cannot avoid risk and hope to succeed greatly, especially regarding financial accomplishment. Risk is an essential part of progress. It is an essential, unavoidable step, along the road to success and wealth.

Therefore, don't focus on avoiding risk, but rather, focus on learning to mitigate and manage risk. That is, find ways to control the downside of risky situations, while not preventing the upside from being as profitable as possible.

By far the best tool I have found to help you manage risk is education. In financial matters, risk is managed by developing comprehensive financial intelligence. In business matters, risk is managed by developing a sound working knowledge of business fundamentals.

It amazes me how many people learn some simple basics about a given field of endeavor, or hear of an opportunity that could yield significant returns, and then jump into a deal with minimal or no education regarding the subject matter. If you want to invest in real estate, you need to learn about the industry, the risks and rewards, how to analyze properties, how to structure win-win deals, and a great deal more. If you want to invest in securities, you need to learn as much as possible about investing, how to minimize your risk exposure, how to select the right professionals to assist you when needed, and how to best leverage your available resources. If you want to start your own business so that you can realize unlimited earnings potential, and so that your creative ideas benefit you and not just an employer, then you need to learn how to evaluate, how to organize, how to manage, and how to drive a business to profitability.

The true vehicles that lead to great personal and financial success typically require a good bit of specialized knowledge, many late hours of study and unpaid work, and character, persistence, and tenacity. But, if you are willing to invest in the proper education and to roll up your shirt sleeves and go the distance, then the risks associated with all of these powerful vehicles, and other pathways to financial success, can be managed and success can be yours.

Many people remain in a job they dislike, or in which their skills are woefully underutilized, because they feel it offers them some form of security. Truly, your only security in the world of employment is in your skills and talents that others would find of value. What is your personal attitude toward job security? How strong are your skills and talents that could be of value in helping you find alternative sources of income should your current employer leave the area or go out of business? How could these talents be used in a part-time way, coupled with leverage, to produce additional income today which could be used to begin building or to accelerate the growth of your wealth portfolio?

DEBT

It is no wonder that most people in society never realize any sizable wealth. Fundamental concepts that form the bedrock of a sound financial success strategy, especially as pertains to wealth, are often misunderstood in today's society. For example, many feel that debt is bad. Nothing could be further from the truth.

Consumer debt, where you borrow money to buy non-performing assets, especially those that depreciate rapidly, such as cars and expensive clothes, is indeed bad. But, properly used investment debt is an entirely different matter. In fact, without employing investment debt to increase your use of financial leverage in the attainment of performing assets, it is unlikely you will ever realize substantial wealth. I have learned to manage the risks and emotions of employing large amounts of investment debt, and actually enjoy watching the money of others build my wealth. Note however that I am careful to learn the strategies employed <u>thoroughly</u> before risking my assets in leveraged opportunities. Believe me, it is worth the effort to learn how to properly employ financial leverage. Once you do so, you will be positively amazed at how fast your wealth can grow!

List all the assets you have purchased recently, such as a car, house, furniture, clothes, and investment assets. Which of these assets actually put money in your pocket on a regular basis, while at the same time growing in value? If you wish to become truly wealthy, the amount you spend on non-performing assets must be significantly less than the amount you invest in performing assets that appreciate and yield positive streams of passive income.

INVESTOR-HEAD OR
CONSUMER-HEAD?

In the highly popular book, *The Millionaire Next Door*, the authors provide a large amount of evidence that shows why many in our society are unable to achieve any measure of wealth. It often comes down to their attitude with regard to investing versus consuming. Many spend the majority of their earnings to fund a lifestyle well beyond their means, and as a result never set aside money to invest. They focus on consuming rather than investing for the future, and often mentally fool themselves into believing they are financially successful because of the beautiful environment they build around themselves through this hyper consumption. They have become what I refer to as "consumer-heads" rather than "investor-heads." Many even take this financially destructive behavior to the extreme, not only spending all of the liquid assets they have in order to fund their hyper consumptive lifestyle, but also using expensive credit to further fuel their spending habit.

The bottom line is you must become an investor-head instead of a consumer-head if you are to realize financial independence. When you have excess funds, you should determine the best use of those funds, carefully considering your long-term objectives.

It is amazing how many people, when they obtain a little extra money, immediately think of buying a convenience item, such as a television or new car, without carefully considering whether they can truly afford the item. More importantly, they don't consider the long-term cost of the decision. In other words, most people are programmed as consumer-heads instead of investor-heads. If you wish to achieve any lasting measure of financial success, your thoughts must constantly revolve around how you can best make use of available funds, including funds from others, to generate a larger base of performing assets that will generate greater and greater amounts of profits for you and your family. You should always think as an investor-head and do all that you can to avoid the consumer-head mentality.

There is a well known saying regarding this consumer-head mentality called "keeping up with the Joneses." As you likely know, this refers to the way many people focus more on creating an image they want others to see, an image that might lead others to believe they have more than they actually have, than on truly developing a strong personal financial base. It is far more important to focus on the right things, and to make the absolute best use of each dollar you have at your disposal, than it is to create a fictitious image of success that has no real basis in fact. When you turn out the lights at night to sleep, you know the facts, and if you wish to rest comfortably, you must be comfortable with reality.

Consider the following example of consumer-head mentality. John lives in a small house that desperately needs repairs to ensure it maintains its value. These repairs include replacement of rotting wood, new paint, a new front door, updated heating, and several other essential repairs. Keep in mind that John's house, if properly maintained, is a valuable asset that can facilitate his borrowing money for future investment. Additionally, his house will likely appreciate in value, in the process yielding several other positive benefits. If his house is not properly maintained and is allowed to deteriorate significantly, it will not appreciate but may indeed depreciate significantly in value. John also drives a used, but dependable car needing new paint and a few minor repairs.

John's great aunt, an elderly lady of substantial financial means, passes away and leaves $15,000 of her estate to John. As soon as John receives the unexpected inheritance, he immediately considers how best to use the funds. Before long, he finds himself at the local car dealership, where he begins looking at used cars. John correctly realizes that buying a new car is often a way to toss good money out the proverbial window, so he looks for a quality second hand vehicle in excellent condition. He settles on a pickup truck and immediately orders upgrades to install expensive chrome rims, tinted windows, special shocks, extra wide tires, and several other improvements. He has one of the hottest trucks on the block, but still lives in a house that is rapidly losing value from physical deterioration that could be readily fixed using just a portion of John's recent inheritance.

John has focused on having a better vehicle and creating a better image, worried more about what others think than about his true financial condition. He figures no one will see his house, and besides, most of his friends live in similar houses, with major repairs needed but neglected. He fails to realize that protecting the value of his house will help him have more financial security and will move him forward toward the dream of wealth which he often considers in his private moments. Yes, John feels a sense of accomplishment and pride from his decision, and he enjoys the positive comments that his consumer-head friends shower upon him. But is it worth the true price? John doesn't understand the ultimate price of his decisions, and doesn't take time to learn how to properly use the resources he has at his disposal. Whereas investing in his home, or even better, investing in his education, would have been much wiser choices for his inheritance, John made the wrong choice. He made the consumer-head choice that our society encouraged him to make. He made the choice that reflects the basic reason why many in our society remain financially poor with opportunity all around them.

If you dream of financial freedom, you must immediately begin focusing on eliminating your tendency to fall prey to the consumerism trap. Do not let the daily bombardment of television commercials, glitzy ads, and store displays pull you away from your focus on investing for your future. If you truly program yourself to always look at every use of money as a potential investment waiting to happen, you will find it more and more difficult to waste money on consumer items that will just lose their value.

With the proper focus on conserving your dollars and minimizing your expenditures on consumer items, you will have more to invest, more to leverage, and you will realize far greater returns than you ever thought possible. Remember, you can only leverage that which you possess or have access to. And the more you have to leverage, the faster your performing asset base will grow.

One final point you must appreciate. Opportunities to realize wealth producing rates of return on investments often arise unexpectedly. You cannot wait until an opportunity presents itself to begin building your asset base. You must begin right where you are today so that when opportunity presents itself, you are in a position to capitalize thereon.

Do you have a well written personal financial statement that lists all of your assets and liabilities? If not, you should develop one today. If you do not have one, visit www.KeyBI.com for a free template you can use to help you put this incredibly valuable document together. As you complete your financial statement, carefully consider the consumer debt you have incurred versus your investment debt. Investment debt is debt used to purchase assets that grow in value whereas consumer debt is debt used to purchase assets that decline in value. For example, debt used to purchase a car or consumables such as food and clothes would be considered consumer debt. Debt used to purchase investment real estate would be investment debt. If you ever wish to become financially free, you should strive to have zero consumer debt and to intelligently employ investment debt for growth. Ask yourself, am I a consumer-head or an investor-head?

FAILURE

Although this book is about leverage, it is necessary to briefly discuss the concept of failure, for as you begin changing the way you view the world, and as you begin to branch out and employ leverage, you will experience setbacks and emotional challenge. You must understand this is not failure.

Indeed, failure is perhaps one of the most misunderstood elements of success, and it is the fear of failure that often prevents those understanding the basics of leverage from employing it.

I have personally had many setbacks and challenging situations that many would label "failure." For example, in honoring an eight year old commitment, I started a division in one of my companies, and then brought in a friend that, contrary to initial indications and screening results, was unqualified for the position to which he was appointed. My friend then proceeded to bring in others who were equally unqualified to fill the positions they were given. Ultimately we were not able to achieve the level of success we initially sought in this division. Before we spent excessive capital, most of which I financed, I had to close this division of the company, in the process laying off my friend and numerous employees. Contrary to what most would feel, I don't view this as a failure. Instead, it was a valuable learning experience. By ignoring warning signals I should have heeded, and in an attempt to honor an old commitment that should have no longer applied, I led or agreed to place numerous individuals in management roles which they were ill equipped to fulfill, thereby possibly dampening their desire to step out and risk it again. But at the same time, they learned some incredibly valuable lessons which will benefit them tremendously if they use the knowledge as a learning experience. It would have been very easy to throw in the towel, but I have learned that failure is nothing more than a stepping stone to success. I never once considered our activities a failure. Instead, I considered them a test, a learning experience through which I was able to learn incredibly valuable lessons I could have never learned from a book. By reframing what initially appeared as a failure, and by looking for opportunity within the crisis, our company is realizing the start of much greater success than could have been achieved in three years on our initial path.

The fact is many businesses experience challenging times early in their lives as they tweak their direction and find their true path. Often, this is accompanied by a corresponding negative balance sheet, often in excess of $100,000. It is the business owner or leader that understands the need to reframe challenges into positive learning experiences that truly succeeds long-term.

Herb Truce once said, "What people don't realize is that successful people often have more failures than failures do. But they keep going." In fact, have you ever met a truly successful person, or wealthy person, that has not experienced some form of setback? If you have not already done so, then research one of the greatest examples of persistent effort in the face of apparent failure, leading to great success. Research the life and career progression of Abraham Lincoln. You'll see what I mean.

IT DOES NOT REQUIRE MONEY!

Let's discuss another myth that holds many back from outstanding financial success. Many people have said to me, "I can't invest in real estate. I can hardly pay the bills and I don't have any money to invest!" And the sad thing is they truly believe this. Again, it is due to incorrect programming.

It is impossible to employ leverage on assets that you don't have. But there are many ways to raise investment assets or capital. In the case of real estate, there are many investment opportunities where you need no cash to buy investment property. For example, refer back to the true story of the $17,000 house discussed earlier.

The key is to have the desire. If you have the desire to pursue knowledge, and to find others who are successful and willing to work with you, then you can find a way to reach your goals. It is not easy, and it requires diligent persistence, but it can be done.

For example, let's look at real estate. If you really learn how to qualify opportunities, and then you diligently work to find opportunities and put winning deals together, you can readily find money partners or investors with the financial resources to invest with you to make it happen. Remember, the use of money to buy investment real estate does not mean it has to be your money.

Additionally, there are many properties that can be acquired without the use of money. For example, there are properties available with seller financing, where the seller finances the purchase for you, and there are a variety of ways you can buy properties with other creative methods requiring little or no cash from your own pocket.

Finally, there are legal, time proven ways to quick turn investment real estate making profits without ever taking title. You can then use part of those profits to fund your operation, with a shoestring budget, while you focus on creative strategies to minimize the actual cash you have to invest to build your portfolio.

The lack of money is not a valid excuse to stay away from opportunity. You can obtain money to invest if you adopt the correct focus and if you take time to truly learn how to qualify and structure investment deals.

DIVERSIFICATION

Listen to many financial advisors and you will continue to hear, "Diversify, diversify,

diversify." Then look at what one of the wealthiest men in history, Andrew Carnegie, had to say on the subject. Carnegie insisted that you should "Concentrate; put all of your eggs in one basket and watch that basket." This is not diversification, at least not the way most define it.

So, is diversification a bad thing? Not necessarily, but if your goal is to far exceed the average in terms of wealth, then you must diversify differently than the average person. Do the rich diversify when they're trying to build their wealth? Yes, but not in the same way the typical middle class investor does. Perhaps they diversify in typical manner once their wealth is established and they want to lower risk and put things on autopilot, but while they're building their wealth portfolio, they focus heavily on those select and targeted things that generate wealth producing rates of return. A basic rule of wealth is that when you are just beginning on your wealth creation journey, you concentrate. Don't dissipate your energy in a dozen different directions. Pick a few targeted strategies destined to create your financial bedrock, and pour all your talent and energy into maximizing the use of leverage to yield the greatest returns possible. Keep in mind, you should keep some reserves on hand to prime the pump again if things don't go as anticipated.

Please note, I'm not saying that diversification is a bad strategy, and that it doesn't have a place in your plan. But it must be used properly, at the right time, and in the right way. Diversification is a method of lowering risk. Keep in mind that there are other ways to minimize risk, the most important being proper knowledge. Once you have financial independence, and you decide to lower your risk as you place your financial life on autopilot, then diversification may be a larger part of your strategy.

Many financial advisors target their advice around those strategies most suited to the general population. And the general population knows little about wealth generation, about risk mitigation strategies, and about investing and leverage. Therefore, they promote diversification for everyone they meet. If you're reading this book then you likely recognize that you must adopt a different strategy than the masses if you wish to succeed greatly.

Diversification also is a concept that, in a general sense, goes against leverage. To take maximum advantage of leverage, you must focus on those vehicles that can give you the leverage you need to reach your goals. You need to concentrate your forces, whether they are time, money, or knowledge, on maximizing the use of leverage, while at the same time using intelligence, and properly selected risk mitigation tools to protect your position.

A note of caution is in order. If you are concentrating your efforts and financial reserves in very limited, highly leveraged vehicles, the risk is greater, in some cases much greater. You should only invest in this manner once you have thoroughly learned your vehicle of choice and once you have learned how to protect yourself as much as possible from major losses. For example, if you're investing in the stock market, you need to understand long and short positions, and how to use buy and sell stops, and perhaps options, to protect yourself from damaging losses.

Keeping in mind the above discussion, it is important to note that there are some highly focused ways to diversify which you can employ, once you begin to accumulate assets. For example, if you invest in securities, once you develop sufficient amounts of money to invest you might build a portfolio of carefully selected stocks across a range of industries to diversify your holdings. This is in a sense your own mutual fund, but it is one that you can carefully control and is thus a form of focused diversification.

Perhaps you are building a real estate portfolio of residential properties. You can spread your portfolio across several locations, thus taking advantage of geographic diversification. You can diversify the types of financing you use on properties, depending on how long you wish to hold the subject properties. And finally, you can diversify the different types of properties you are holding. Again, this is a focused type of diversification that fits well within the leverage concept, but that generally requires you first have some assets in place.

HIGH RATES OF RETURN REQUIRED

Tell the average investor or even the typical financial advisor you wish to develop a sizable nest egg in twenty years. Then ask if you should be happy with an average of 20% return per year on your investment portfolio. He'll likely say, "Yes!" But ask a person who has achieved outstanding financial success, and he may very well give you a different answer. You see, depending on where you are in life, 20% by itself may not be enough to produce outstanding wealth, the kind of wealth that can change not only your life, but also the lives of countless others through your efforts and generosity. To really achieve your greatest potential, you must find vehicles that can provide wealth producing rates of return. The closer you are to your target date for financial freedom, the faster this rate of return must be to reach a given target. This may mean taking some risks and making liberal use of leverage. It is very difficult to realize wealth producing rates of return without the use of leverage, and most likely in all its various forms.

One of the most incredible leverage vehicles available to you is the leverage of time coupled with compound interest. Go back and review the concept of compound interest and the formidable returns that can be realized over time. When comparing various scenarios using a compound interest calculation model, look at the difference resulting from higher rates of return. If time is short, then the rate of return must be high, if you are to realize significant wealth accumulation.

Suppose you have $10,000 to invest and you

wish to turn this into a million dollars in ten years. What rate of return will you need? Well, $10,000 compounded at 20% will only yield a little over $30,000. I think you'll agree this is hardly a wealthy sum. How about 30%? This yields slightly less than $70,000 after ten years, still a small sum by today's standards. What about 50%? Well, now we're making progress, with a ten year result of a little over $430,000. But we're still shy of the mark. To reach your goal, you must realize a 70% return on investment. That's an example of a wealth-producing rate. And that is a rate of return that is almost certainly going to require the use of leverage, if you plan to have easily reproducible and consistent results. Indeed, the proper, careful, and consistent use of leverage can accelerate many investments to the wealth producing speeds you need.

THE WEALTH TRIPOD

Stand two wooden legs on end, with the upper points connected, and they will likely fall. Add a third pillar so that you have a tripod, and if properly positioned, it will stand strong and tall. This is how I like to think of wealth building. There are three vehicles well suited to take maximum advantage of leverage, and when you put the three together, they can rocket your efforts for wealth and success forward at a remarkable pace.

The three incredible leverage vehicles I have found particularly well suited for generating wealth producing results are financial investing, real estate investing, and building business systems, especially those which integrate the power of technology into their core business model.

Some of the late night infomercials would have you believe that establishing one or more of these vehicles is like taking a pill and waking up the next day rich. It does not work that way! If it did, we would all be financially independent. However, if you apply yourself, are willing to take risks, are willing to be reset to zero both emotionally and financially, and to start over, possibly more than once, then you can establish these three pillars of wealth, and ultimately, personal and financial success for you and your family.

Allow me to share some of my personal experiences with you. I began working in corporate America as an Associate Design Engineer making $28,000 per year, after having spent nearly five years in engineering school at

NC State University. I had at the time already been working with my dad in real estate for several years, and had begun a part-time network marketing business, with positive results. Interestingly, it wasn't long after I began my first network marketing business that I figured out what I truly wanted to obtain from it. I didn't want to get rich from this endeavor, but rather I wanted to learn about the business. During the day I worked as an engineer. At night I learned business, studied, and over time experimented with other businesses. I have experienced many temporary setbacks, some years in length, and I have learned some incredible lessons that are paying healthy returns. It was hard work living a double life, but it taught me lessons I could not have learned otherwise.

I originally planned on working for larger companies for approximately 10 years to gain the knowledge I needed to assist me in achieving my life mission. I ended up staying in corporate America for approximately 13 years, after which I chose to make the break and focus on my own companies, in part because it was costing me too much to remain in the employment of others. My sideline activities were growing my wealth far faster than my corporate employment, and being an employee allowed me little time flexibility to grow my leverage vehicles. I now enjoy freedom and flexibility that many only dream of, knowing that I am in control of my destiny to the maximum extent possible.

To truly learn how to build these three pillars you must couple study with application. You will make mistakes along the way. You will invest a lot of time along the way. And you will possibly lose money along the way, perhaps more than you think you can stomach right now. But the rewards are worth the risks, provided you go the distance.

As you read and study, consider why these three pillars work. Also, as you read, take time to contemplate what you're doing today, or what you can begin to do, to help you build these pillars for your financial future. Once you have some ideas in hand, take action to convert your ideas into reality.

Consider the difference between a self-employed business owner running a shop individually by himself and a leverage based business system. What are some of the primary differences between a business system employing time, knowledge, and financial leverage and the typical small business owner's operation?

FINANCIAL INTELLIGENCE

Let's consider an example which illustrates the importance of sound financial intelligence. As you read this example, consider the saying "A fool and his money are soon parted." Early in my professional life, I had some extra money to invest. I knew about real estate but knew little about investing in the financial markets. I was setting aside money in my employer's 401(k) plan but was not receiving wealth producing rates of return. I sought out a few successful individuals, and one put me in touch with a securities broker that had helped him realize excellent returns on his investments. Aaron, the broker, worked diligently for me, and his recommendations yielded significant returns on several occasions. After a few years working with Aaron, I began to follow his recommendations almost without question and violated one of the rules I now follow -- to never let someone else be responsible for my money. On his recommendation, and over a quick phone call, I invested in two IPOs (initial public offerings). The amount invested wasn't huge, just $15,000 or so per IPO, but what happened next had a huge impact on my subsequent investment decisions. A week or so later, I called Aaron and said, "Well, I guess we need to find somewhere else to put that money back into play." You see, the stocks had declined rapidly in value. In approximately one week my investment had gone from a collective value of approximately $30,000 to a value of around $2,000. My standard practice in risky stock plays such as this was to implement steps to protect my capital in the event a sudden undesired shift in the stock value occurred, typically through the use of stop orders. In this case, I did not verify my order was in place. I assumed it was done, but it wasn't in place and the money was gone! I made one of the critical mistakes so many make, blindly entrusting their money management to someone else. I trusted Aaron to help me make decisions and to trade for me. As a result of not carefully managing my own money I had lost approximately $28,000 in one week!

When a stock you're holding decreases in value, the monetary value of that stock, and hence your available money, has dropped and it is a REAL loss. It may come back, but if you had converted it to cash before it dropped, you'd have that much more to invest. Don't play mind games with yourself and convince yourself that a stock which you hold and which has drastically dropped in value is not really a loss. It is. Your decision to keep your money tied up in such a stock should be based on tax consequences of selling and on your use of the money. If there are better investments, warranting the taxable loss if applicable, then take what you have left and put it in play. Money invested in a dead stock that is down for the count is an example of lost opportunity.

Along this same time, I changed my local financial advisor to Jacob, a young gentleman who came highly recommended. I shifted a portion of my assets into mutual funds recommended by Jacob. Soon afterwards, the stocks in the mutual funds began a rapid slide downward. Jacob recommended staying in as the stocks therein were "high quality." Additionally, he also had a fairly large investment in these same funds. You can likely guess the story. The mutual funds were soon down for the count. I experienced the money I had invested in the funds recommended by Jacob performing a six figure disappearing act in approximately six months.

Before these events, I had been toying with the idea of spending around $3000 to take an intensive weekend training camp on stock market investing. I had previously considered it too expensive, but now I realized that it could save me a fortune and help me improve my financial intelligence. So, I attended the next one in the area. I learned what I had done wrong, and more importantly what I should have done right. Thereafter I spent late nights studying and paper trading in stocks and options. I learned how to thoroughly analyze a company and a market segment, and how to properly isolate the best investment opportunities. I learned the ins and outs of fundamental and technical investing. And then, when I knew that I had a workable approach and that I understood what I was doing, I began massaging my portfolio and carefully trading with real dollars. Now, my portfolio is filled with a small group of carefully selected securities that are traded when the time is right, using short sales and margin to maximize leverage. By carefully investing in the right stocks, and by holding them for just the right amount of time, I have been able to boost my stock portfolio returns to as high as 30% yield per quarter.

Opportunity exists all around you, even when everyone else is preaching how bad things are. An expert investor can make money when a stock moves up and, interestingly can make money even faster when a stock moves down.

The key is financial intelligence. Many people are fairly oblivious to the rules of money, understanding little more than how to write a check and balance their checkbook. They understand little or nothing about the financial investment vehicles available to them. Rather, they blindly trust someone else to make their financial decisions for them. If you want to succeed financially, you must learn the strategies that lead to financial success, and you must assume personal responsibility for your own financial growth.

The first criterion for gaining financial intelligence is to understand how important it is. Then, as stated before, you must allocate some time and money to gaining this intelligence. Tune into educational programs on television, attend seminars, and read educational books. Seek out knowledgeable individuals who demonstrate an in depth understanding of both traditional and non-traditional strategies for maximizing your financial development. Learn as much as you can so you can properly evaluate the information you obtain. Keep in mind that not all you read will put you on the right path. Screen what you read carefully because you are highly influenced by what you feed your brain.

Finally, before leaving this topic of financial intelligence, let me just share another example of how to combine more than one leverage vehicle in a win-win fashion.

A couple of friends of ours have a son, Timmy. Timmy is not only incredibly intelligent for his age, but he is also a highly motivated young adult, in search of knowledge to put him on the path to success.

As I have knowledge, and Timmy has time, we are considering a win-win agreement. I will teach Timmy my investment strategies, how to evaluate the market, and how to perform basic fundamental and technical analysis. I will provide tools with which he can track these investments, and will provide guidance on how to interpret the information he gathers. He and his dad are then going to take some time each day to research investments, are going to track the opportunities they uncover, and are going to present summaries to me, on which I will make the final decision for investment. I will put $10,000 of my money up as seed capital, and now with every profitable investment, Timmy will get half the profits and I will get the other half. Not only is Timmy going to potentially make money in his spare time, but he is also going to begin building his own investment portfolio with the returns, will be investing in his education, and will be opening the eyes of his family and friends in ways they have never been opened before. At the same time, I will be using the information he provides to make ten times the return through other accounts, leveraging in a truly win-win fashion not only his time, but also my money. Again, it's about looking for opportunities, finding new rules with which to play the game, and being willing to take a little risk.

I'll share another true life situation in which I am leveraging the time of others in a win-win fashion to help me grow the value of my securities portfolio. Occasionally I am asked to speak at schools on stock market and real estate investing. After one such discussion at a local high school for gifted students, I met with two of its recent graduates, both exceptionally gifted individuals. They asked me to help them establish a stock market investment portfolio. I agreed to fund a small portfolio in exchange for their researching and managing the portfolio under my direction. I loaned them an in depth home study course from my personal library and then explained various strategies I've used successfully in the market. I will keep half the profits generated by our mutual activities and they will share the balance of the profits. Their likelihood of success is much greater working with me than it would be if they invested alone, and I am able to make more accurate investment decisions with their research assistance than I would be able to make without it.

Before moving past this section, let's discuss the topic of mutual funds. In my humble opinion, after having tasted success in one of the most turbulent markets in history, and after having learned to successfully employ wealth principles, I believe traditional mutual funds are, for the most part, the investment vehicle of average investors. You see, there is another critical element to successful financial investing, other than focus as mentioned before, and that is control. You must be in control of your money if you are to succeed in your wealth building endeavors. You must also have options and the ability to take advantage of opportunities regardless of which way the market is headed. You want to be able to profit when the market is going up, and when it is going down, which is often not the case with many traditional mutual funds. Also, with many mutual funds, you have little or no control over when capital gains taxes are realized. And what a pity it is to have your money spread out so much that you cannot take maximum advantage of the thousands of targeted, highly profitable opportunities that present themselves everyday. If you haven't already done so, learn the basics of investing in securities directly, the basics of mutual funds, and the basics of self-directed traditional and Roth IRA's, especially those allowing non-traditional investments allowing you to realize maximum control and use of leverage.

If you have a self-directed retirement account, such as a traditional or Roth IRA, you can utilize a custodian that allows a much wider variety of investments than the typical custodian will allow. Your IRA can invest in private notes, real estate, and other leveraged vehicles that provide wealth producing rates of return. If you haven't done so before, seek out information and learn about these non-traditional custodians. One such company is Equity Trust Company, which can be found on the Internet at www.trustetc.com.

Chapter Six

Risk

"Risk and reward go hand in hand. Life is inherently risky. It is those who seek to avoid risks at all costs that ultimately assume the most risky position of all."

— Ron D. Pate

RISK

Any discussion of leverage would be incomplete without discussing risk. Risk is indeed a factor that many never seriously consider or understand, yet it is an integral component of any use of leverage. Although we touched on risk in an earlier section, let's discuss it further.

Fear, stemming from the desire to avoid risk, keeps many from venturing into the areas of life and business that truly have the potential to help them realize their dreams, particularly their dream of financial independence. But what most people fail to realize is that risk avoidance is also risky, as the avoidance of risk is also the avoidance of opportunity. And further, people fail to realize how risky life itself actually is. In fact, as long as you are alive, you're exposed to risks.

The successful and wealthy typically have a different attitude toward risk than the general population. They work hard to understand the risks to which they are exposed, and then they work even harder to find ways to mitigate the risks, or develop strategies to deal with any outcomes that might take place as a result of the risks to which they're exposed.

Risk mitigation is typically much more productive than risk avoidance. Perhaps the most important tool for mitigating risks is knowledge. For example, investing all of your available funds without proper knowledge, and without financial intelligence, is a high risk proposition indeed. But investing with proper knowledge, and with the proper risk mitigation steps in place, can yield significant positive results, even though risks are present.

Risk mitigation can take many forms. For example, insurance is a risk mitigation strategy. So is the use of corporate entities to shield you from personal liability, and the use of corporate entities or trusts to compartmentalize investments.

Let's consider another example. I have numerous companies in which I buy and hold investment real estate that is in turn rented to residential and commercial tenants. When I purchase investment real estate, my corporate entity buys the real estate, versus me buying it personally, thus shielding me to a great extent from personal liability. I then go one step further. In addition to having a corporate entity hold the real estate, I also insure the real estate, both for property loss and for liability protection. If the property burns down, the insurance will pay for replacement of the property. If someone sues the property owner, my company, then liability insurance will kick in and cover the first $2,000,000 awarded, before they can attach to any of the assets held by my company.

Likewise, I hold personal umbrella liability insurance just in case someone is hurt at my personal residence and chooses to sue me as a result. My insurance will pay any claim that may arise, and this amount must be consumed before my personal assets are placed at risk.

There are various other risk mitigation strategies. For example, when I invest in real estate, I do so using various forms of focused diversification. These include geographic diversification, diversification of the financing used on the property to match the hold time expected for the particular investment, and property type diversification.

If you're investing in stocks, you can use buy stops and sell stops, as well as options, to protect yourself in whatever position you may acquire. If you don't understand securities, put this on your list of personal objectives. If you do understand securities, then you should understand these methods.

Carefully consider your risk tolerance and feelings regarding risk. Are you fearful of risk? On a scale of 0 to 10 where 0 represents complete risk avoidance and 10 represents reckless abandon with regard to risk, where would you place yourself? Does your attitude prevent you from taking advantage of opportunities that might lead you to the success you desire?

AVOIDING OPPORTUNITY

Many have what it takes to achieve their dreams but lack the willingness to assume the risks that go along with opportunities for significant accomplishment. Yes, risk must be realistically assessed, and hard choices must be made with careful consideration and serious commitment. But, the willingness to take manageable risks can ultimately lead you to great rewards.

Let's look at an example. Bill used to work for a large corporation, until his position was eliminated in the early 2000's. Unfortunately this came at a time when Bill and his family were in a significant financial crisis brought about by unrelated circumstances. Bill viewed this as an opportunity rather than a crisis and never missed a beat. He formed his own company and with faith and a strong commitment to succeed set out on a path that many considered much too risky.

Today, just a few years later, Bill has restored his family's financial health, and is on his way to realizing his dreams of financial accomplishment. Had Bill not taken the path most considered too risky to take he might still be looking for a job. Instead, today he is on his way to becoming financially free and is inspiring many others during his journey.

So, don't try to avoid risks at the cost of missed opportunity. Instead, learn and study what risks you are exposed to and develop strategies for dealing with and managing these risks. Only then can you maximize your use of leverage for success.

Are you one of the many people who have dreamed of becoming an entrepreneur but that have never taken the first step? Is risk avoidance holding you back? How might you start your own part-time business, mitigating risks that you'd be exposed to if you were to make a clean break to full time entrepreneurism?

Chapter Seven

Technology
and the
Information Age

"Technology is one of the greatest leverage
tools of all time. Explore, embrace, and
master this powerful tool!"

— Ron D. Pate

INTERCONNECTED LEVERAGE VEHICLES

The use of knowledge leverage is interconnected with two other forms of leverage, time and technology leverage. Therefore, although this chapter focuses on technology leverage, you will see time and knowledge leverage at use in this chapter. Technology offers perhaps one of the most exciting forms of leverage in existence today.

The terms knowledge leverage and information leverage are sometimes used interchangeably, although knowledge is a different concept than information alone. With the growth of technology providing more and more powerful ways to utilize information and knowledge, technology based leverage opportunities are increasing at an explosive rate.

GO WITH THE TREND

Every several hundred years, society goes through tremendous shifts. The last shift was when we moved into the industrial age, which went on for hundreds of years. Today we are at the beginning of another shift, from the industrial age to the information age. These shifts bring about massive changes in developed countries, and create tremendous opportunity for those who recognize what is happening and find ways to leverage the opportunities around them. Coupled with the shift to an information-based society is an unprecedented increase in the sophistication and application of technology.

One way to increase your leverage in situations is to get in front of trends. As it has been said, "the trend is your friend." Just as moving with a trend can help you greatly in your journey of success, trying to move against the trend can be devastating. For example, I recently met the owner of a growing insurance agency. He started his career using paper-based systems for managing his business, and continues to do so today. He seemed to be proud of the fact that he never checks his email and that his office is not really focused on using technology for growth and profitability. When I asked him some pertinent questions, he admitted that his franchise headquarters had sent him an important email that he never received, and as a result some fairly important negative consequences arose. Hopefully he will realize that his company's continued growth will be jeopardized if he does not adjust his business practices. Another company I had a chance to work with recently had a large office, with fancy tables and lots of sales professionals, and yet all of their computers were totally disconnected from one another. They were using a shared phone line for Internet access, tying up their fax machine access whenever someone was online. Interestingly, another client of mine had considered giving this company an order for approximately $100,000, but as this client embraces technology and customer service, they decided to go with another provider. This client told me because they could never get through to this company, and because they couldn't email the company and obtain prompt responses, they went elsewhere. This company could have purchased new computers, equipped and networked everyone in the office, and provided top of the line training to all personnel for less than they lost in profits on this one order.

You must recognize and embrace the information explosion trend, and the corresponding changes in technology. Failure to do so will greatly reduce your ability to succeed now and in the future.

Of all the forms of leverage that exist today, knowledge leverage, driven by information and technology changes, is perhaps the most exciting. Interconnectivity trends, such as the growth of wireless communications, are creating truly remarkable shifts in our world. As the integration of advanced and relatively inexpensive technology permeates our daily lives and rewrites our lifestyle trends, it will create unprecedented opportunities for astute entrepreneurs to employ knowledge leverage for massive success. Although it will be those who learn how to take advantage of these opportunities in new ways by "thinking outside of the box" that will see the greatest rewards, even those who join existing trends and do a few things right can realize incredible success.

In addition to the trends noted above, what other trends are affecting our society? How might you leverage these trends to further you along your journey of success?

USING TECHNOLOGY LEVERAGE

Let's look at a few examples of how technology leverage, specifically technology designed to drive the flow of information or knowledge, is being applied for success. Keep in mind the examples given here will be expanded many times over as these incredible and unstoppable trends progress.

Nearly everyone has heard of online auctions. I personally enjoy buying and selling items in online auctions, using no leverage since I consider it a hobby. But I have met various successful individuals and studied numerous cases where online auctions have resulted in incredible financial returns to online marketers.

Let's consider Robin. She started out as the office manager of an industrial supply company. After realizing the incredible leverage that online auctions offered her, she was able to transition from her job to a business of her own. She began by creating a simple, but neat information product, mostly composed of information and links to freely available software people could use to format their own auctions. She began selling these on eBay, not sure what the results would be, and within just a short while had sold almost 200 copies at $10 apiece. Keep in mind that her cost was less than a dollar per copy.

She continued to create additional information products, all very simple to compose, and found ways to package them to increase the value realized by the buyer. Soon she began realizing an incredible return on her time and efforts.

The leverage here is in the power of an automated system, through which Robin exposes her offerings to millions of people, many who can use and benefit from the product she provides.

What other examples of automated systems based on new technology can you think of? Do these systems represent any type of leverage? For example, consider an ATM machine. Instead of the bank employing a teller to perform the function of the ATM, an automated device interfaces with the bank customer. This is an example of time leverage through the use of technology. Time on the part of someone was employed to develop and install the machine, and someone must maintain it, but the overall time required by the bank employees or contractors is drastically reduced.

Now, consider how leverage vehicles can be combined to further increase her opportunities for greater and greater benefit. Perhaps she could hire students from a local high school as a part of a cooperative program to gather and create the materials, and then have them perform the auctions, with her receiving a percentage for her expertise.

If you work in a modern office, you'll quickly spot many other ways that technology is being used to increase the flow of information, and to increase the pace at which business and life in general take place.

One problem that arises is that people do not adapt their methods to match the trends occurring around them. For example, with the increase in activities and the increase in information, an increase in the ability to be selective and organized is needed. Professionals in sales and other highly interactive roles who try to remember every commitment and appointment and ignore the need for organization quickly become overwhelmed. As a former sales executive and sales manager, I was able to maintain a very fast pace, accomplishing a great deal more with my time than did many of my peers. I did this by focusing on ways to increase my productivity by adopting techniques for managing information that flowed my way, and by standardizing workable systems for maintaining maximum productivity. Not only did I seek to perform the activities I engaged in efficiently, I also employed technology leverage to assist me in creating new levels of productivity. For example, whereas most professionals in similar roles were using paper-based systems for tracking their activities, contacts, and so forth, I adopted an electronic personal information manager which integrated seamlessly with my email and other computer based records. This allowed me to realize not only tremendous increases in my output, but also to provide even greater customer service to our clients than others were providing. By moving from a paper-based planner to a computerized organizer that "connected all the dots," I was able to quickly update my schedule, to copy over pertinent records from email, and to set automatic alarms to notify me when a commitment was forthcoming. I could quickly update and duplicate contacts, and could share information with others with the touch of a button. As an interesting side effect, whenever I was with clients, they recognized my highly effective information management methods, and when I freely shared these with them, they did their best to give my company business. In a sense, this too was a form of leverage, as the use of the systems I already had in place to assist others resulted in new, unanticipated benefits when my clients tried to assist me in return even though my intent was simply to be helpful.

And the list goes on and on. The key is to think creatively about win-win possibilities, and ways in which you can combine the sources of leverage at your disposal. For example, the Internet offers you the ideal tool for combining knowledge and technology leverage. There are vast amounts of information resources on nearly every conceivable subject freely available on the Internet. When you search and find information that assists you in achieving your goals, you're actually leveraging the knowledge of others, and by using the Internet, you are employing technology as an enabler of knowledge leverage application. The key to effectiveness here is to be selective. Learn how to use the Internet to accomplish specific tasks, and remember to use personal discipline in using this tool, so that you're not distracted and wasting valuable time that could be better spent on other activities.

Let's consider another example. Assume you have developed a collection of outstanding recipes and you know, without a doubt, that many would greatly enjoy the delicious dishes you've created. You find a local high school student who has spare time to type up your handwritten recipes. It takes this student 20 hours to type the recipes, and you agree to pay him $10 per hour for his time to do so. During the time he is typing the recipes, you are working on new recipes which will yield far greater than $10 per hour in value. This represents a total direct cost of $200. You then buy an inexpensive software application for less than $100 that will convert your Microsoft® Word document into the popular Adobe® Reader® portable document format. You now have your new book in a format suitable for electronic distribution. You also download Microsoft Corporation's free application to create a Microsoft® Reader® format e-book, now allowing you to provide your book in two easily readable and popular formats.

In order to promote your new book, you decide to set up a nice, easy to use website. You find a web hosting company that will host a suitable yet inexpensive website for you, including a simple shopping cart for processing online orders. Using the shopping cart frees up your time to focus on more intellectual property development, increasing your overall output significantly. Then, you find an individual who is knowledgeable in web site development and optimization for search engine placement. Your total cost to get your website and storefront online and properly positioned on the Internet is approximately $3000. Let's assume you don't have enough money in hand to cover this bill. You work out a win-win agreement with the developer that he'll get a percentage of the profits from the venture. You guarantee that he'll receive at least $1500, regardless of how well the book does. If it does well, he'll receive a percentage of the profits, up to 300% of his initial $3000 quote. The upside of this arrangement far outweighs the downside, and it furthermore places the contractor in a position to really want the book to do well, which ensures you will receive his best effort and attention on the project. Your site does not have to be a high-end, graphically intense site. Rather, it is a simple, easy to understand, pleasing site, designed to deliver significant value.

As a part of the book purchase, you offer a referral program to your readers so they can help you spread word of your new book. Now, you've not only leveraged the power of the Internet to reach millions, but you've employed the oldest sales method around -- word of mouth. Let's go one step further. Suppose you give free license for others to put a link to your book on their website, so you can create a virtual web on the Internet pointing right back to your leverage vehicle. Have you noticed how many people and businesses are establishing websites these days? Note that numerous online sites have applied this concept successfully.

Finally, you find a few dozen ezines looking for attractive content and you offer to provide them content in exchange for a small ad in each ezine. Since these ezines are sent to tens of thousands of qualified recipients, you're able to achieve a great deal of publicity for your new book with very little of your own time and effort. Technology has allowed you to realize a tremendous time and knowledge leverage benefit.

Do you see what we have done? We've taken tools that already exist and created a leverage vehicle, in this case, a vehicle for marketing your knowledge automatically, 24 hours a day, seven days a week, with little of your time required to manage the sales process. And, even better, we've established a win-win environment where everyone benefits. Consider that there are literally hundreds of millions of people on the Internet every single day. Of course, you can't just hang out your shingle and expect them to flock to your virtual door. Like any other business, making money from the Internet requires diligent effort coupled with thoughtful planning and execution.

Not only is leverage possible with information-based technology, but other forms of technology as well. For several years I worked in a factory where electrical transformers are manufactured. During this time, numerous forms of technology were implemented in the factory that vastly increased not only the quality of product produced, but also the amount of product that could be produced per man-hour of effort. This is a common type of technology implementation blending time and technology leverage for vastly greater outputs. Perhaps one of the most visible forms of this type of technology implementation is in the use of robots for automobile assembly.

If you're serious about leverage, then you must take time to learn how to leverage the Internet. Learn to leverage other forms of technology as well, especially information based technology. You may very well realize results that pleasantly surprise you.

There are many inexpensive, quality reference sites on the Internet that will help you learn how to structure money making leverage vehicles like the simple example noted above. You should seek out and become familiar with these sites.

Visit your favorite search engine and search for lists of ezines. Find several that interest you and see if there is a way you might leverage these ezines to generate passive income with a little creativity on your part.

Again, we are in the beginning stages of a **tremendous shift**, a shift to a technology enhanced, information driven society. You cannot change it, so embrace it. Seek opportunities to apply leverage brought about by this shift to help you achieve massive success. Learn as much as you can about the use of technology in modern society and ensure you stay on top of developing technological advances which are shaping our society.

How familiar are you with modern technological advances and technology in general? Do you use computers or PDAs to help you accomplish more in your line of work? Are you using them effectively? How might you better leverage the technology that surrounds you to free up your time and increase your output?

Chapter Eight

A Strong Foundation

"Any true lasting success is built upon a strong foundation exemplified by life balance, outstanding character, thoughtful planning and diligent action."

— Ron D. Pate

A STRONG FOUNDATION

As we have discussed, leverage is an incredibly powerful tool that allows you to vastly increase the yields you realize from your efforts or investments. It is the fundamental principle which forms the base of all powerful wealth development strategies, and it is used by nearly all who achieve seemingly impossible success in short periods of time. Indeed, if you are to achieve the maximum success and wealth possible in your life, you MUST employ leverage.

However, when it comes to the use of leverage to accelerate you on your journey of success, caution is in order. Just as a physical lever requires a strong fulcrum, or foundation, if it is to be useful in moving heavy objects reliably, you too must have a strong foundation in place before you attempt to employ leverage in your own life in any appreciable manner. The use of leverage without the proper success foundation in your life may not lead to true success, fulfillment, and happiness.

In fact, the use of leverage may benefit you little, or even worse, can lead to personal distress and frustration if you do not have a solid success foundation in place first. For example, if you have poor financial habits and begin investing heavily in real estate with little experience and training you could end up facing foreclosure and bankruptcy as have many unwary investors who were enticed by questionable get-rich-quick programs. If you question that the application of leverage in significant ways without sound success basics in place first can lead to negative circumstances, consider the many entrepreneurs who launch their dream company with little idea of how to run a business. Many invest their entire life savings and then go bankrupt in the first few years of operation. Or consider famous celebrities who demonstrate various self destructive habits even though they have tremendous wealth and opportunity at their fingertips.

Therefore, let's look briefly at what it takes to form a solid foundation on which you can build your leverage vehicles for success.

THE MOST IMPORTANT FIRST STEP

It is amazing how many people never determine exactly what they want out of life; exactly what it is they desire to have accomplished when they're at the end of their years. They have dreams, but they never seriously consider exactly what they wish to accomplish and why. Yet, this is the single most important thing anyone wishing to achieve any lasting measure of success and fulfillment must determine.

Unless you know what you're living for, it will be difficult for you to reach your true potential. You must determine with absolute certainty what your personal mission during this life is, and you must write it down and focus on it intently, day in and day out. If you do nothing else as a result of this book, do this. Think, really think, about what you want most to accomplish during your brief stay in this world. It may take you a while to nail it down, but once you truly figure this out you'll know it in your heart, and your life will never be the same. This one step can lead you to a more successful future than many ever realize.

Do you have a passionate and inspiring mission for your life? Is it written down? If not, take time to carefully reflect upon and write down your own personal mission statement. If you have a mission statement already, reflect on this mission statement and consider what updates might be appropriate. Remember, your mission must excite you if it is to pull you forward. Your mission provides the foundation on which all of your life success will be built.

STARTING POINT

Many people develop goals for their life, and regardless of how hard they work, find they still fall short of their goals time and again. This may not be because they didn't know what they wanted, but rather because they didn't realistically assess where they were to begin with, and because they were overly ambitious due to a lack of realism and self-understanding. One of the first things you must do after you determine what it is you want out of life is to assess where you are now. What is your starting point? Take for example the person who dreams of becoming a professional singer, but who only sounds good in the shower. This aspiring singer needs to truly assess his or her skills, in objective fashion, and to define what strengths and weaknesses he or she possesses which need to be shored up or enhanced if the dream is to be realized. In other words, a realistic self-assessment is in order.

To enhance your own self-understanding, consider your own strengths and weaknesses. What resources do you have at your disposal, not only in the way of financial resources, but also connections, talents, and desire? What immediate opportunities are present which could possibly open a door to the achievement of your dreams? What threats exist with which you'll have to deal if you are to achieve your goals in life? If you are to develop a path to success, you must have a clear picture of where you are now so you can pave the road from here to where you want to be.

Be careful when soliciting the input of others. For example, family and friends tend to often complement young people on talents such as singing or dancing when singing or dancing may not truly be talents the individuals possess. This is likely due to the desire most people have to not hurt the feelings of others. When it comes however to charting your course through life, you need to have a realistic assessment of the personal resources at your disposal. Be sure you are listening to objective feedback before putting substantial resources at risk.

Write down your personal strengths. What opportunities do you have to improve or utilize those strengths to move you forward on your journey of success? Also write down your personal weaknesses. What threats to your success do these weaknesses pose? What strategies can you develop to overcome these weaknesses? Take plenty of time and revisit the results of this exercise frequently. This is a highly useful tool for helping you reach your dreams.

ROADMAP

Once you know for certain and have written down in the form of a personal mission statement what you wish to accomplish in life, and once you have realistically assessed where you are to begin with, the next step is to define a roadmap; a game plan for reaching your goals and dreams. Don't be like many people who just wander through life with "pie in the sky" dreams, never taking time to develop concrete time driven goals and objectives to give themselves a realistic chance of success. If you wish to use leverage, or any other tool for success, you must develop a life plan. Your plan should begin with your personal mission statement followed by major life goals, long-term and strategic in nature. These are followed by shorter term, more tactical goals; perhaps on a one to six month basis. These goals are then followed by specific action steps you can take on a daily basis. Carefully think through HOW you're going to accomplish these goals and objectives. What people or resources are needed? Exactly when will you reach these goals? Why are they important?

No ship's captain would launch from port to travel across the ocean without a detailed plan and compass. Likewise, you should not try to navigate your life without a plan and direction. The successful individual develops a plan for his or her life and knows where he or she is going. If you wish to succeed, so will you. It is not difficult, but it requires careful reflection and honest communication with yourself. This is the most important thing you can do to ensure your long-term potential is realized.

Do you have written goals for your life? If not, take time to write down at least three important, long-term goals. Break each of these down into shorter term goals and finally, define specific action steps you can take today to help you reach each of your short term goals. Assign a time frame for each and write down the resources you will need in order to accomplish each goal. Develop an action plan for each goal, detailing exactly HOW you will reach it. If you do have written goals, revisit each and ensure it meets the criteria outlined above.

ATTITUDE

After finding your purpose in life and developing a detailed roadmap to guide you toward your dreams, the next most important factor is having the right attitude. Your attitude should be one of positive expectancy coupled with a healthy dose of realism, and a commitment to persist until you reach the success you desire, regardless of what challenges may come your way. You must believe in yourself, and your ability to reach your goals and dreams, without question.

Don't allow short term setbacks and mistakes to get you down. Rather, treat them as learning experiences, which is exactly what they are. Indeed, the truly successful person knows the only failure in life is to quit. Everything else is simply a stepping stone to success.

Don't allow yourself to get pumped up to the point that you begin living a fantasy and fail to realistically assess your current position. Always be realistic, albeit a little aggressive, in your plans and projections. You want your goals to be a stretch, but not completely out of reach. This realism coupled with a positive, win-win attitude and undying commitment to push on until you realize the success you desire is critical.

Carefully consider your attitude. Identify at least one concrete step you can take to improve your attitude. For example, if you always use negative vocabulary such as "What's wrong?" consider alternatives such as "What's right?" Take action to implement this change!

PERSISTENCE

If you ask highly successful people what traits or characteristics they feel have had the greatest effect on their position in life, you'll usually find that persistence is a key ingredient in their success formula. This has certainly been the case in my own life. There have been many times when the amount and size of the challenges facing me seemed insurmountable. Yet, in those times I dug in my heels and refused to give up, and before I knew it the skies cleared and it was clear sailing again. Whenever I feel like giving up I remind myself of the following quote, one of my favorites.

"Nothing in the world can take the place of persistence. Talent will not; nothing is more common than unsuccessful men with talent. Genius will not; unrewarded genius is almost a proverb. Education will not; the world is full of educated derelicts. Persistence and determination alone are omnipotent. The slogan, 'Press on,' has solved and always will solve the problems of the human race."

--Calvin Coolidge

Remember, persistence and determination will take you far in life.

Chapter Nine

A Call
to Action

"Knowledge without application is nothing

more than entertainment."

— Ron D. Pate

YOU MUST TAKE ACTION

In these chapters I have tried to open your eyes to the power of leverage and to encourage you to seek ways to employ leverage for success. No matter where you are in your personal journey of success, there are opportunities all around you to employ leverage. It is my hope that you will take action to seek out ways to use leverage and that you will do so with great expectations and total commitment.

If you do not plan what you want out of life, and seek ways to accomplish it then you will go through life like a boat without a rudder, drifting wherever the winds and tide may take you. But if you do plan your life, work your plan, and employ leverage you can achieve extraordinary outcomes. It has been accurately stated that those who fail to plan actually plan to fail. Consider this carefully.

Remember, no matter how much you learn, until you take positive, concrete action, you will not find the success you seek. Learn, study, and apply the principles you learn. As you apply the principles, you'll be learning through experience, and experience based learning is the absolute best type of learning you can embrace.

EFFECTIVENESS AND EFFICIENCY VERSUS LEVERAGE

Let's briefly revisit the topic of effectiveness and efficiency.

Ask highly successful individuals what tools help them accomplish more than others and they they will undoubtedly mention effectiveness and efficiency. Indeed, to truly realize the greatest success possible, you must be effective, meaning you do the right things, and you must be efficient, meaning you do things in the right way.

Although there may appear to be similarities between these two concepts and the concept of leverage, leverage is a separate and supplementary concept. Unlike effectiveness and efficiency, leverage is about increasing the quantity of output from a given amount of effort, or input, regardless of how effective or efficient a given effort might be. Think about the difference between these three concepts as you begin to employ leverage.

It is important to integrate all three concepts into your actions. That is, always try to utilize leverage effectively and with the maximum efficiency possible. This will ensure that you realize the maximum success possible from your efforts.

SUGGESTIONS FOR SUCCESS

Let's wrap up with some suggestions you can follow to help you begin or increase your use of leverage. If you follow these suggestions they will have a definite positive impact on your life.

1. Reread this ENTIRE book, carefully considering each concept, and making notes in a separate journal on specific actions you need to take to maximize your success.

2.   Review each of the exercises and questions provided throughout the book. Take time to record your thoughts and responses in writing. Visit www.LeverageForSuccess.com for helpful supplemental information.

3. Carefully consider all of the things you do on a daily basis and identify at least ten ways you can employ leverage to increase the yields you receive from your efforts. This might include hiring an assistant for personal chores while you spend the time saved in higher output activities (leveraging someone else's time), hiring an investment coach to help you grow your financial portfolio (leveraging someone else's knowledge), or teaming up with

a money partner on a specific investment to increase the yields you receive from your own financial outlay (leveraging someone else's money).

4. Research leverage concepts on the Internet. Using a search engine, type in phrases likely to yield meaningful results. Try such phrases as "financial leverage," "principle of leverage," "leveraging other people's time," "leverage and risk," and so forth. Much of the information you'll find does little to further your knowledge of the core leverage concept, but you will find some golden nuggets of insight. Not only will this exercise help you develop a greater leverage awareness, but if you're not familiar with using the Internet as a learning tool, it will open the door to this tremendous knowledge vehicle. Remember, like anything you read, screen carefully the information you find to ensure it makes sense.

5. Determine how much money you will need to live on in retirement. Consider how much money you have now to invest. Then find a compound interest calculator on the Internet. Go to your favorite search engine and type in phrases such as "future value

calculator" or "compound interest calculator" to find these sites. Then plug the following variables into the formula: your starting investment, the amount you can contribute yearly to your investments from your earned income, how many years you have until retirement, and how much you need at retirement to live comfortably. If you aren't sure how much you will need, take your current lifestyle annual monetary requirements (your current yearly earnings is a good estimate if you're like most folks spending most of what you make) and divide by 0.07. The result will be the approximate amount you'd need to have invested with a 7% annual rate of return to generate the same amount of income you now live on. Plugging all this into the formula will provide you with a percentage rate -- the rate of return your investments need to yield in order for you to have enough at retirement. Now, to account for inflation, take this rate of return and add some to it. For example, if you feel inflation will average 5% for the things you will buy to live on, then if you had 25% yield, you'll actually need 30% yield to offset the decrease in value due to inflation. The new amount of money at retirement resulting from this new investment yield is the amount you will need in "future dollars" or dollars at the time of retirement. Take time to understand this exercise completely. This is one of the most important exercises you can practice as it clearly shows you the importance of investing for your future, and perhaps even more importantly it shows you that you have no time to waste in getting started. More complex models can be developed for retirement, including varying rates of returns for various investment vehicles, social security benefits, and so forth, but this simple model gives you a good starting point.

6. Pick one or two leverage concepts, and using your own personal examples of their use for greater achievement, teach this principle to one or more of your friends or family, helping them realize how important leverage, with controlled risk, is to greater long-term achievement. You might also teach them the power of compound interest in action if they have not been exposed to it before.

7. Visit the website www.sba.gov. Study what it takes to build and operate a business successfully. Even if you are not the entrepreneurial type and choose to work for

someone else, the study of this site will help you develop a greater understanding of the company for which you work. If you're planning to start a part-time home based business, this site can give you valuable insights to help you be more successful. After you have researched this site, use a search engine to find additional reference material on the Internet to further expand your knowledge.

8. If you are not familiar with real estate investing, pick up a few books to learn how this field of investing has made many people very wealthy. Stay away from the get-rich-quick books teaching you to never get a loan, that you don't need sound financial habits, and so forth. Remember, carefully screen what you read. A good general overview book to begin with is Gary Keller's book, *The Millionaire Real Estate Investor*. Also consider signing up for real estate license training. Even if you don't take the state exam to receive your license, the class will help you learn the rules and regulations governing real estate in your local area. Additionally, you are likely to meet people during your class that could be helpful to you if you pursue real estate as an investment vehicle.

9. If you are not familiar with the use of a computer, and with the use of popular software such as word processors, spreadsheets, and email, then bite the bullet and find a way to buy a computer. Many used computers can be purchased very inexpensively and will work fine for beginners. If you can't afford a computer, visit your local library as many libraries have computers freely available for public use. You can also find reference books at the library which will cost nothing but which will help you embrace the information age we are now entering.

FINAL THOUGHT

The use of leverage has allowed me and many others to achieve outstanding personal and financial success. I am confident that you too can realize greater success in your life through the use of this powerful tool.

Remember that this life is not a trial run and there is no rewind button. It is up to you to take action, and if you do so, patiently and persistently employing the many success tools available to you, you CAN realize your dreams.

May you experience the greatest success that life has to offer!

EXCITING SUCCESS RESOURCES

Visit Ron's training company, Key Business Institute, Inc. at www.KeyBI.com for exciting resources to help you realize your dreams.

Some of the valuable items you'll find here include:

- A list of Ron's favorite personal and professional development books and audios;

- Links to excellent resources on the Internet for helping you realize the greatest success possible;

- Exciting products and training programs from Key Business Institute, Inc. and its affiliates, all designed to help you realize greater personal, professional, and financial success;

- Announcements on upcoming events and product updates for the books and programs Ron has released and is developing to help you realize the greatest success possible;

- A discussion forum where you can post messages and questions and receive FREE advice directly from Ron and his executive team.

REGISTER THIS BOOK!

Please register this book by visiting www.LeverageForSuccess.com. This will entitle you to special benefits including FREE electronic copies of future updates to this book.

TO ORDER

Copies of this book may be ordered at your favorite bookstore, from Amazon at www.amazon.com, from Key Business Institute, Inc. at www.KeyBI.com, or directly from:

VP Publishing, LLC
P.O. Box 4623
Rocky Mount, NC 27803

$14.95 plus $4.00 shipping & handling

For quantity orders please send your inquiry to the above address, fax your inquiry to 1 (866) 583-2845, or email your inquiry to orders@vppublishing.com.

PASS IT ON!

If you have enjoyed this book and feel the information herein is valuable, *please tell your friends and associates.*